MetaCapitalism

The e-Business Revolution and the Design of 21st-Century Companies and Markets

GRADY MEANS

DAVID SCHNEIDER

Foreword by
JAMES J. SCHIRO

John Wiley & Sons, Inc.
New York • Chichester • Weinheim • Brisbane • Singapore • Toronto

This book is dedicated to our consulting colleagues
at PricewaterhouseCoopers, as well as to the universe
of new warriors at the MetaFrontier

Contents

Foreword

A fundamental transformation of the business model is under way, to which the central precept of Darwinism applies: Companies must either adapt or perish. The book you have in your hands digs beneath the breathless anecdotes about instant success and explosive wealth creation to discover a truth that is at once exhilarating and sobering.

The authors identify an emerging economic framework to which they give the name *MetaCapitalism*. They expect the worldwide business economy to configure and behave in entirely new ways—an astonishing prediction. More astonishing still is their contention that businesses have only the narrowest window of opportunity to remake themselves—at most, a few years, and those years are now upon us.

Some companies are already embracing the e-business revolution and assuming leadership roles in the New Economy. Their instructive and inspiring stories are told here. Other companies—particularly those in traditional heavy industry—have yet to fully leverage the enormous possibilities of Internet-enabled business. But the authors leave no room for doubt that they too must accept the new paradigm, because e-business will transform *every* industrial sector.

While the clock is ticking for every business, the message of this book is exciting and optimistic. It foresees a world in which the business-to-business e-business revolution will sweep every corner of the economy, where the supply chain will be dramatically streamlined, where tremendous efficiencies will be attainable, and where worldwide capital market value will explode.

The opportunities for companies with the financial means and human and intellectual capital are manifest. The key is to know how to leverage those assets in time to ride the wave into the e-business future. No mere exercise in futurism, this book is a survival guide for the New Economy, an invaluable road map of the digital landscape.

I urge business leaders, entrepreneurs, educators, legislators, and public officials to absorb its chief findings. The transformation of the global economy will have profound social and political implications. MetaCapitalism will literally change our world. I invite you to read on and discover how.

James J. Schiro
CEO
PricewaterhouseCoopers

Acknowledgments

The development of the basic draft of this book was quick (two months), virtual (many contributors worked online with the authors), and "meta" (ideas were reviewed, refined, and discarded or adopted over short periods of time by an ever-changing set of teams).

Contributing to the overall content of the book, Michael N. Bazigos was tireless in assembling and structuring the material. Robert Avila, an outstanding economist and business forecaster, developed many of the most insightful ideas and forecasts for the book. Michael Hanley helped sharpen our focus and direction. Ric Anderson performed a "technology and value chain sweep" to ensure the accuracy and focus of our technology discussions as well as improve the overall content. John Jacobs and Peter Davis provided pragmatic senior executive business insights that strengthened many chapters.

In preparing the discussions of business-to-business e-business and MetaMarkets, the authors drew heavily from the work of Matt Porta, Rory Jones, Karin Blair, Philip Landler, Rich Krigger, Amy Wright, Patrick King, Bill Bound, and Bill Battino. Each of these consultants has thorough experience in guiding major corporations toward successful e-business strategies. Collectively, they have created a virtual encyclopedia of new business concepts associated with the Internet and business-to-business e-business.

Roger Heijens, Don Schulman, Frank Milton, and many others helped us better understand the new business processes associated with MetaMarket companies.

Industry examples matter in this book, and we had the help of many contributors to get them right. Special thanks go to J. Ferron and Dave Garfield for their insights on the automotive industry; Jill Kidwell for her extensive work on higher education; Mark Austen for framing our views on financial services; Bob Reeve, Colleen Wesling, and their associates for their insight into MetaMarket solutions for government; Mark Kingdon for his insights into virtual retail companies; Joe DeVittorio for his expertise on the chemical industry; and many others.

We are indebted to the e-organization consulting team of Dexter Hendrix, David Tunney, Steve Ulene, Raj Chinai, Giri Giridharan, David Boatright, Anjali Vichare, Kristen Gemeny, Jeff Petee, and Mohan Sriperambadur for huge insights and assistance in writing the section on "bubble in, bubble out" approaches to organizational transformation.

To articulate the new economics of MetaCapitalism and apply options theory to its dynamics, we were supported by some of the most outstanding practitioners in the field, notably Adam Borison and his associates at Applied Decision Analysis in Stanford, California. Jack Dunleavy also deserves special thanks.

John Kopeck and Mike Briglia helped us keep well in mind that traditional valuation concepts such as free cash flow have not gone away.

As we articulated strategies for moving management forward to business-to-business e-business, we benefited from the insights of Bill Trahant and other members of the Change Management team. We are also mindful of the research contributed by members of the Strategic Change team: John Carr, Radhika Philip, Kyung Nam-Wortman, Roy Lubit, Michael Fang, Jeffrey Plein.

Adam Tinkoff, a wizard of digital media, directed the preparation of charts. Carol Marek demonstrated the true meaning of e-sweat as she prepared and typed the manuscript.

At John Wiley & Sons, we were grateful for the warm welcome offered us by Lawrence Alexander and his team.

Finally, this book would never have reached publication without the great support and nearly tireless guidance of our in-house editor, Roger Lipsey; the encouragement and contributions of our partner, Joel Kurtzman; and the enthusiasm of Bill Dauphinais— our partner, nay our Virgil, as we explored the Net world.

A final word, to acknowledge a market reality. Because stock markets *will* rise and fall, we want to make clear that the thoughts in this book are not tied to the Dow, NASDAQ, Nikkei, or any other market index. We are confident that the new MetaCapitalist design of companies and markets in the twenty-first century will produce astonishing expansion and wealth. But securities markets worldwide will naturally remain volatile, nervous. Many new MetaCapitalist ventures will be created. Some will succeed, many will fail, all will reflect attempts at real transformation and progress. Our book points toward a new and incomparably more successful model for businesses worldwide. But as we write in later pages, there are risks ahead and there will be stumbles. This is not bad. This is what markets do. MetaCapitalist markets will do it faster *and* better.

Grady Means   David Schneider

Introduction

$$e_{(b)} = M(C)^2$$

A worldwide earthquake is shaking the foundations of traditional economic and business thinking. And for once the results of a quake are good. It is generating a tidal wave of economic growth and prosperity, changing not only business but also politics and international relations. Economic value and wealth creation will accelerate to unprecedented levels. Global capital market value will grow from $20 trillion to $200 trillion in fewer than 10 years, unleashing undreamed-of possibilities and solutions to longstanding problems. This book documents the early tremors.

Moore's law (the power of information and computer technology grows exponentially as its cost diminishes) now applies to economics and business conditions as much as to technology. Worldwide economic conditions and frameworks change ever more dramatically over ever shorter periods of time: This is Moore's law in its broadest application. *The period from 2000 to 2002 will represent the single greatest change in worldwide economic and business conditions ever, and most of the impact will occur during the next 18 months.* If companies (and countries) do not change their assumptions and strategies during the next 12 months, they will almost certainly fall behind and probably be left behind.

The key driver of this change is the business-to-business (B2B) e-business revolution. But the strategic principles underlying the change and the formulae for business and economic success are not

just technological. Their roots lie in a vast array of changes that
have occurred over the past 20 years—among them:

- Globalization of the world economy and the integration of
  worldwide capital markets through widespread privatization,
  lowering of trade and capital barriers, and the development
  of global market and investment strategies
- Dramatic restructuring of companies over the past 20 years
  through business process standardization, simplification, and
  refocusing under the rubrics of cost reduction, business
  process reengineering, supply chain synchronization, Enterprise Resource Planning (ERP), and customer understanding and management
- Increasing installation and reliance on technology for business management, based on the economics of Moore's law
  combined with the year 2000 (Y2K) threat and the growing
  power and usefulness of technology applications—leading to
  a transformation of business systems
- Growing acceptance of the need to focus on core business
  skills and processes and the resultant movement toward spinning off or outsourcing noncore processes
- Exponential growth of business-to-consumer (B2C)
  e-business, accelerating use and acceptance of the Internet,
  and the rise of e-retail and e-finance as accepted consumer
  activities

The era we are moving into—the B2B revolution—will transform the leading companies in each industry worldwide and force
them to compete in entirely new ways that take advantage of this
vast array of changes. Competition will be characterized by the
emergence of brand-owning companies that devote their energies
to meeting customer requirements and driving product innovation. They will be allied with companies that focus on key parts of
the supply chain and demand chain. Efficient supply chains will
support deeper levels of customer satisfaction, while demand
chain activities will also increase customer satisfaction through

e-supported customer relationship management. Far more than at any time past, competitive pressure to assure customer ownership will drive intense and continuous optimization of markets, responsive operating and backroom processes, and the continuous refinement of marketing and customer ownership strategies. Companies will be forced to innovate continuously and to transform regularly simply to keep pace with this intense level of competition. Economic growth and value creation will accelerate to unprecedented levels. The stock market valuations that have been common in B2C .com businesses will become common across the major industrial and financial services sectors. And all of this will be bought at a price: The required speed and flexibility of response will demand huge changes and an entirely new level of management competence and discipline.

We term this massive business and economic transformation *MetaCapitalism*. It will sweep the world in the next few years, triggering enormous economic growth and value creation and changing many of our fundamental assumptions about wealth creation and distribution. Unless corporate leaders fully understand these trends and the principles underlying them, they are likely to be unprepared for the transformations required by B2B e-business.*

The first glimmerings of this revolution are just becoming evident. Internet-based companies, which created valuations that were hard to understand during the business-to-consumer period of the past few years, are now joining major industrial and service companies in launching the B2B revolution. This will lead to an even more dramatic increase in corporate value—which will again be hard to understand and digest on the basis of conventional business principles. We are, at least temporarily, in an uneasy zone of paradox: The market is not wrong, *and* most traditional principles of business management still hold true. Tremendous imagination and

---

*While this book deals with B2B e-business and intersections among allied companies and industries, many of these processes are closely linked to B2C processes. In effect, many of the changes noted in this book are business-to-business-to-consumer (B2B2C). Overly fine distinctions would be misleading and are not intended.

insight, combined with courage and an occasional leap of faith, are needed to enter into and succeed in this new world of virtual business and virtual economics.

$e_{(b)} = M(C)^2$

MetaCapitalism requires a new math. We need to move from the arithmetic of business to something closer to relativity theory:

$$e_{\text{(business-to-business)}} = M(C)^2$$

A well-intended corruption of Einstein's classic equation for the relationship between energy and mass (energy equals mass multiplied by the speed of light squared) turns out to be a highly useful metaphor in understanding the new mathematics of e-business:

Business-to-Business e-Business
= Management (Change × Courage)

In short, to create new B2B e-businesses that overtake the leading incumbents in *every* industrial and service sector requires a management team that:

- has enormous insight into the *changes* that have occurred over the past 20 years and will occur over the next 2 to 10 years, and the imagination and instinct for innovation that will allow them to design entirely new approaches to business based on these new principles
- has the *courage* to launch a total transformation of their companies over the next 12 to 18 months, to build on the changes of the last 20 years and take advantage of today's B2B revolution, thereby positioning their companies to benefit from the "disruptive technologies" and economic changes that will surface over the next four to five years

(As a parenthetical comment, we want to add that *management* refers not only to corporate and business management, but also to the management of public institutions. Political and public leadership based on insights, courage, and political skill will be necessary to lead countries and public institutions wisely through these transformations. Leadership of that quality will make the difference between countries whose economies grow successfully and those that do not.)

To extend the relativity metaphor a little farther and apply it to MetaCapitalism:

- **The B2B revolution will occur at the speed of light.** Major companies in every sector will transform from the conventional to the e-business model over the next 12 to 18 months. New companies will form and rapidly take market share from those that are slow to change. This too will occur in every sector, including all phases of manufacturing, financial services, health care, retail, entertainment and media, telecommunications, and government.
- **"Mass" will be converted into "energy."** The advantages of owning the physical capital of production capacity will be replaced by the need to dominate *MetaMarkets*. What are MetaMarkets? They are outsourced, managed networks that continuously replace elements of the supply chain with more efficient players. Participants at various points along the demand or supply chain will be essentially free agents, easily replaced to improve performance at that point in the value chain.
- **The transformation will shrink both time and space.** The leveraging of the Internet to create closer integration of supply chains and operating networks, global access to markets and suppliers, global communications across management teams, and the growing use of information exchange using broadband techniques will allow institutions to serve worldwide customers and use a global supplier network—from their desktops.

- **The market will accumulate mass exponentially.**
  Worldwide capital market value expanded tenfold from $2
  trillion to $20 trillion in the period from 1980 to 1999. The
  enormous leverage created by the factors of change outlined
  above and consolidated by B2B strategies should increase
  capital market value another tenfold to $200 trillion over the
  next 8 to 10 years. As in the relativity equation, time accelerates—$(c)^2$—and shortens the period for reaching higher
  valuations and earnings multiples because of greater capital
  leverage (financial, human, and brand capital). The Dow is
  likely to continue to expand dramatically, and the world is
  likely to experience an unprecedented expansion of economic value and wealth—books forecasting a 36,000 or
  100,000 Dow argue among other things that the market is
  well below proper value in light of the transformations now
  approaching. Like nuclear fusion, MetaCapitalism creates
  continuous reactions along the value chain and can be
  expected to create value and release energy for decades. The
  implications of this growth, not just for the developed
  economies but for developing economies, will be dramatic.
  (In a sense, the right law to apply here is not Moore's, but
  Metcalf's: The value of a network increases by n^2 with the
  number of players in the network.)

The Internet leverages financial capital, as well as human, intellectual, and brand capital, on a worldwide basis. This is reflected in
the unprecedented growth and value of the .com companies,
which still today represent only a tiny fraction of the economic
value and wealth creation possible through B2B transformations.
As major industrial and financial institutions "decapitalize" and
leverage MetaMarkets on a scale that dwarfs the B2C enterprises,
the economic disruption (in a positive sense) and expansion will be
enormous.

This level of change challenges even the most sophisticated
managers and management teams. The purpose of this book is to
propose frameworks for thinking about this transformation and for

incorporating those frameworks into corporate strategy, decision making, and processes for management change. As with any revolution, or any exploration of a new universe, participants cannot help but experience tremendous excitement, and they will encounter very real risks. They will feel as if they are stepping off a cliff. The enterprise will require expert business skills, a taste for risk, and no small amount of confidence to succeed.

There are only a few central ideas in this book, which is intended as a strategic primer for management rather than an exhaustive review of B2B. But we are well aware that some elements in the pattern of MetaCapitalism are complex. This is not of our doing; we simply try to reflect the emerging pattern of the New Economy. Network technology, building on other major changes of the past 20 years, does appear to be producing enormous new economic growth and wealth. In addition, because of its ubiquity, anonymity, and accessibility it is creating a new meritocracy in which skillful players from all corners of the world begin to compete with far less restriction than ever before. Network technology also provides the greatest opportunity in recent memory for developing nations, and we sincerely hope that our book finds an audience in countries where the fear of a "digital divide" is strongest.

To take a page from *Star Trek*'s Gene Roddenberry, we may be on the verge of moving from the *realm of necessity* to the *realm of surplus and freedom*—from an economic version of violent adolescence to productive young adulthood. We may be poised to create a better worldwide balance of productive capacity and wealth, to move from competition for survival to competition for the earned privilege of defining future cultural models that include business and economic models and much more. As the tycoon in the movie *Contact* said to the Jodie Foster character before she was launched at warp speed to Vega: "Wanna take a ride?" Of course we do—it's the most exciting ride around.

1

The Business-to-Business e-Business Revolution Begins: The "Decapitalizing" of Traditional Companies

As we interviewed chief executive officers worldwide in many different industries for our recent book, *Wisdom of the CEO* (John Wiley & Sons, 2000), we were struck by their similarity of perspective. These were, to say the least, independent-minded men and women, influential thinkers and doers—yet looking at their

1

worlds, they saw much the same things. They all recognized massive forces of change that had gained strength in the past several years. They were all preparing for still more change, driven by the Internet and e-business and building on the forces of globalization, capital markets integration, process simplification, and industrial transformation. This chapter summarizes their thinking, which we found enormously stimulating, and the principles underlying their strategies.

Figure 1.1 represents the prevailing model for major business enterprises of the past 20 years—and, in reality, the past 100 years. Companies have had a large base of physical capital. The asset types have varied as widely as business itself: manufacturing sites, distribution centers, branches of financial institutions, hospitals or health care facilities, retail outlets, telecommunications infrastructure, cable TV systems, entertainment production centers, and so on. Managing these assets effectively in the past 20 years has called for tremendous focus on building or integrating domestic and global operations, streamlining supply chains, integrating with supplier bases and distribution networks, standardizing and improving business processes, installing related technology, and generally improving operating performance and efficiency. In parallel, financial managers have focused on improving return on capital, return on

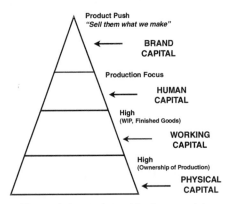

Figure 1.1 Traditional business model.

investment, EBITDA, asset turns, and other measures of effective management of broad capital bases. Industry consolidation has, among other things, involved the consolidation of domestic and global physical capital to achieve scale economies and align physical capital with markets served. The latter has shortened time-to-market for new products and enhanced customer responsiveness in traditional products.

Companies in the 1990s also focused intently on more efficient use of working capital (ingredients, raw materials, parts inventory, work in process, finished goods) with the objective of increasing inventory turns, lowering the carrying cost of inventory, and improving the efficiency of fulfillment systems to decrease product obsolescence and increase customer responsiveness. Key performance indicators have tended to focus on throughput, inventory turns, capital efficiency, and working capital as a reflection of the growing efficiency and responsiveness of supply chains.

To a large degree, the tremendous focus on the more efficient use of working capital in the 1990s was a result of a major economic shift in the 1980s. Prior to the 1980s the real cost of capital tended to be negative or zero for several decades. In essence, the real interest rate on capital (nominal interest rate minus inflation) tended to be zero or negative because of the high levels of inflation. Under these conditions, with the exception of some amount of product spoilage, obsolescence, storage cost, etc., working capital was virtually free; the carrying charges on raw materials, inventory, work in process, and finished goods were essentially zero or negative. Among managers there was, accordingly, little emphasis on productivity improvement or better management of working capital through reducing inventory, improving transportation and distribution, reducing warehousing for finished goods, or any other major initiative of the type launched in the 1990s to better manage and reduce working capital.

Figure 1.2 shows the sudden onset of real interest rates in the 1980s and 1990s, which changed all of this. Companies now faced real costs to their operations, and this abruptly generated awareness that owning and managing all of the factors of production, with their attendant working capital demands, might no longer be the preferred economic model.

Company employees—human capital—in the 1990s tended to concentrate on the factors of production. Process models looked carefully at all elements of the supply chain: sourcing, manufacturing, distribution, supply chain–related financial accounting, new product development and product introduction through company supply chains, marketing and promotional alignment with the supply chain, and integration of selling with the supply chain.

Looking back again to Figure 1.1, we want to highlight one further feature of the century-old way of doing business. Although in recent years there has been a growing emphasis on customer requirements and customer responsiveness—in effect, on brand capital—the predominant focus of most major companies has continued to be product development, manufacturing, and sales "push" to customers rather than customer ownership and customer "pull."

In short, the financial, operating, and business process model for most companies has been based—intuitively or explicitly—on a

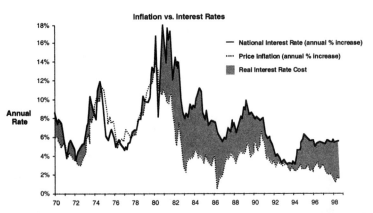

Figure 1.2 The U.S. capital market restructuring and the 1984 recovery hit companies with real costs . . . and focused attention on lean processes and the supply chain.

concept of the enterprise as a physical asset-based pyramid organized to produce and sell products. Recent investments in technology (e.g., ERP and Customer Relationship Management [CRM] systems) have been designed to facilitate this business and process model and to provide tools for understanding and managing it better.

During the late 1980s and 1990s, initiatives to improve and synchronize the supply chain assumed that there was great advantage in having many of the factors in the supply chain under company control, often within its "four walls." Companies worked somewhat independently to identify and design the best supply chain and process models and were most comfortable when they controlled them end to end. The ERP wave changed this view somewhat, by applying a consistent process model to companies in specific industries. During this wave of effort, many major companies achieved a best practice model for internal processes, and some degree of process standardization appeared in many industries. Toward the end of the 1990s, most companies were still working hard to organize and control their supply chains and install ERP and CRM systems to better manage their processes.

However, a rapid and dramatic revolution was already under way. In our conversations at the end of the 1990s with CEOs of major companies, they indicated that the market was no longer rewarding the traditional style of company as richly as in the past. All responsibly managed companies were pursuing greater speed and responsiveness—but the financial multiples for traditional companies were dropping dramatically below the multiples of companies that had successfully leveraged new e-business technology. The e-business companies were proving to be more nimble, and they were achieving greater capital leverage.

For the most part, as Figure 1.3 indicates, CEOs now feel compelled to transform their companies from the conventional business model to the decapitalized e-business model illustrated on the right. In order to better leverage their capital and focus on core competencies, brand-owning companies are determining how to

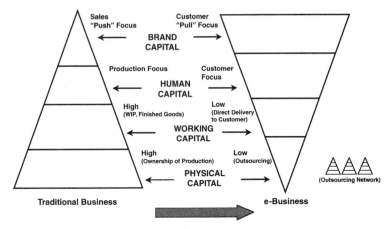

Figure 1.3 The transformation to B2B e-business.

rely less and less on an internal base of physical capital. Instead, they adopt the strategy of outsourcing noncore physical capital activities across the supply and demand chains and outsourcing support functions as well. The B2B e-business model tends to split companies into relatively low-capital brand-owning companies on the one hand and, on the other, companies clustered around these brand-owning companies in external or outsourced networks. The networks provide the supply chain, demand chain, and support services—such as financial processing, accounting, technology, human resources—for brand-owning companies.

A low-capital brand owner operating in close cooperation with an outsourced network is a new business phenomenon, which we term a *value-added community* or VAC. Further, the dynamic relationships among contiguous VACs create a still larger entity, a *MetaMarket*. These new elements and their dynamics—the decapitalized brand owner, the VAC, the MetaMarket—are the focus of this book.

Accompanying the dramatic effort to lower the base of physical capital and outsource is an equally dramatic effort to lower working capital. As brand owners outsource parts manufacture, physical product systems, and large chunks of final assembly for their proprietary designs and branded products, they keep little if any manufacturing inventory in-house. To the degree that they do manufacture, they may focus on highly specialized subassemblies or focus on simply doing kit assembly of a few large systems and subassemblies supplied by their outsourced network. In short, large manufacturers become systems integrators of larger, separately assembled subassemblies. In many cases, they may move to manufacturing nothing at all and have finished products shipped by their outsourced network to their fulfillment centers or directly to consumers. Clearly, spinning off manufacturing and related operating processes, generally to an outsourced network, frees up enormous amounts of capital that can be focused on brand development, customer ownership, supply network management, and other industry leadership processes.

These trends have been evident for some time. In recent decades, for example, the issue of whether to own, lease, or rent has become familiar in organizations of nearly every size. Make versus buy versus rent has become a common decision point. Much physical capital that was historically owned by corporations is now leased; in high tech and .com companies, much is rented. Microsoft, "the most valuable corporation in the world," has but a few million dollars in fixed assets. What, then, does a corporation need to own?

The trends have been evident for some time, but they are now changing the rules across a broad front. In this more aggressive climate, the familiar no longer drives businesses. Standard accounting and financial measurements no longer tell the whole story. The application of capital internally to manufacturing, service delivery, or infrastructure upgrades may be a grave strategic error. Conventional performance metrics related to throughput or inventory and asset turns within the four walls are less relevant. Human capital is focused more on customers and leveraged more effectively to drive growth.

Similarly, brand capital is developed more effectively to retain customers and derive far greater revenue from new channels to customers. Business-to-business disintermediates many non-value-added processes and allows customers to better access and leverage the supply chain. Business-to-business companies can take advantage of this by offering superior access and responsiveness to these customers and creating stronger ties—all of which adds to brand capital.

Business processes have less of an operations character and answer instead to definitions such as "rapid alliance development," "outsourcing and MetaMarket management," and "customer channel management." Investments tend to focus on customer ownership, customer management, brand ownership, and related marketcentric requirements. And the market tends to reward with high multiples those companies that have the flexibility and discipline to master these skills.

It is no exaggeration to say that for the B2B company an entirely new business model is required, with entirely new definitions of business processes.

An example of this dramatic transformation is readily available in the auto industry. For the past several years, the industry has concentrated on improving its supply chains, reducing time-to-market for new models, and increasingly integrating global operations. The auto industry has also experienced tremendous consolidation as the major companies have begun to merge and the number of original equipment manufacturing (OEM) brands has been reduced to a shorter list of nameplates. At the same time, the industry has become more detached from its dealer networks, and this has given rise to the growing phenomenon of megadealers who offer products and brands from many different automotive manufacturers.

Further dramatic shifts are occurring, as suggested in Figure 1.4. The OEM model, represented on the left of the diagram, is rapidly transforming into a vehicle brand owner (VBO) model. Major manufacturers (such as Ford, General Motors, and Daimler-Chrysler) are moving to outsource much of the manufacture of the parts and subassemblies of their vehicles. At the same time, there has been growing interest in investing downstream in distribution and dealer networks.

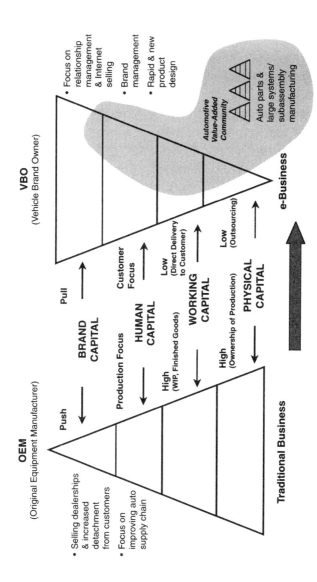

Figure 1.4 Auto industry B2B.

These shifts reflect the reality of the auto industry, in which very little profit has been made in recent decades on the cars themselves (the most profitable product has been light trucks). Servicing and repair, the aftermarket, and related businesses such as auto finance have been the principal moneymakers. Thus, it has increasingly made sense to transition major companies to the role of VBO. As such, the companies may outsource manufacturing, create new alliances and supply chain networks, manage outsourced relationships, and focus on customer responsiveness, vehicle design, distribution, service and repair, and the aftermarket. At the same time, auto manufacturers are learning to use the Internet as a major consumer communications and sales tool. The market is increasingly recognizing these transformations—and beginning to reward them accordingly.

The other link in this story is the creation of the automotive VACs and MetaMarket. To attack this problem, there are at least two broad approaches. Some automotive companies are using technology to create a captive network of suppliers for parts and subassemblies, as well as other products and services. The network is, by definition, closely tied to the company. It can use Net-based tools to cooperate on product design and specifications. It can also bid on additional work—for example, to produce products and services for downstream elements of the supply chain, to supply the brand-owning nameplate manufacturer, or to deliver original equipment or aftermarket services directly to the consumer. The network is knit together by various supply and purchasing technology tools that exchange information, conduct bidding processes, and integrate the supply chain for manufacturing and delivery.

Automotive companies that use similar technology but do not require a fully captive supply base represent an alternative approach. In this model, design and subassembly specifications are provided through a more open communications and network approach to a broader set of potential players. This open architecture model allows a vast array of manufacturing and service providers to participate in bidding and to compete furiously with each other on the basis of traditional measures such as reliability, quality, and price as well as new performance measures such as the ability to interface with MetaMarket technology, fit quickly and easily into the virtual supply chain, and create and dissolve business alliances efficiently.

As these concepts are currently evolving, some automakers have joined together to form a multicompany supply network with common standards. The next chapter will elaborate more fully the concept of auto industry VACs and MetaMarkets and discuss their dynamics.

As we said at the outset, the transformations we have begun to explore in this chapter continue the natural evolution of corporate structure over the past 100 years. This is worth examining more closely. For example, consider the evolution of the automotive industry, evoked in Figure 1.5. After the turn of the century, the archetypal automotive manufacturing operation was Henry Ford's vertically integrated River Rouge Ford Plant. Raw materials (raw steel, lumber, leather, etc.) entered one end of the plant and new Fords came out the other. As in much of the century that followed and in every industry, the focus was largely on design and manufacture rather than customer responsiveness. The familiar motto ran, "Any color you want, as long as it's black." Black had been selected not because research suggested that consumers preferred it. Interestingly enough, it was not even the cheapest color to apply to the car—it was one of the most expensive. It had been selected on the basis of operations efficiency—clearly, an internal focus. Black was the color that dried fastest and kept the assembly line moving quickly, thus creating operating results that were attractive to the production and distribution divisions.

As Figure 1.5 indicates, specialization began to creep in over the years and most of the auto companies created a separate parts division or divisions to focus on subassemblies associated with engines, transmissions, brakes and suspension, bodies, interiors, electronics, and other major subsystems. Over time, as outside suppliers arose with attractive technologies and efficiencies, the automotive manufacturers began systematically to use these sources to compete with or replace their in-house supply base. This prefigured the pattern that is emerging so strongly today. Today the vehi-

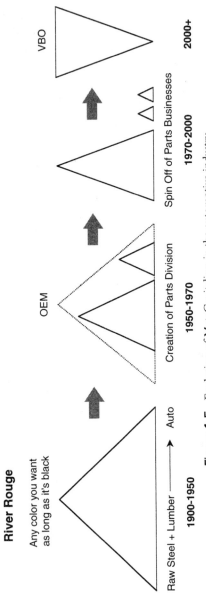

Figure 1.5 Evolution of MetaCapitalism in the automotive industry.

cle brand owner will increasingly rely on large-scale sourcing and purchasing MetaMarkets, while it focuses its own energies on those parts of its business that earn the highest market rewards and maximize value.

The automotive example reflects events in every other industry. Over the next few years, B2B capabilities will transform leading companies in every sector. The dynamic MetaMarkets that are evolving around these companies will allow competition to take place at the "molecular" level of business—the level at which discrete players in the supply chain can optimize from the perspectives of speed, flexibility, cost, reliability, and the ability to quickly integrate with the MetaMarket. We advance the term *MetaCapitalism* for the underlying economics of this B2B e-business transformation. Succeeding chapters of this book explore how MetaCapitalism will transform the competitive fabric of every major sector of the economy and dramatically change our assumptions about economic growth and value creation.

Well, what about those assumptions? Will the transformation to thinly capitalized brand-owning companies, which coordinate complex outsourced MetaMarkets, create an explosion of economic growth and wealth creation? We believe that this point can be argued from realities rather than from suppositions. A case study to which we will periodically return provides a persuasive example: Cisco Systems. In Chapter 3 we will outline some of the underlying management approaches and business processes of Cisco Systems. For present purposes, we will simply use basic balance sheet information to illustrate the multiplier effect and power of Meta-Capitalism.

Figures 1.6, 1.7, and 1.8 illustrate the relative levels of capitalization (physical capital and working capital) at Cisco and several competitors as a proportion of the total enterprise. The charts highlight a distinction between Cisco Systems, developed on a MetaCapitalist model, and its three most successful competitors: Not only does Cisco work off a proportionally smaller base of physical and working capital, but it also strives continuously to reduce that base.

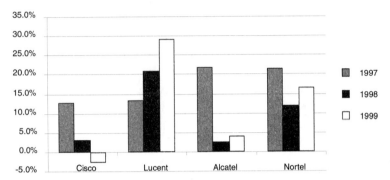

Figure 1.6 Net working capital/total assets.

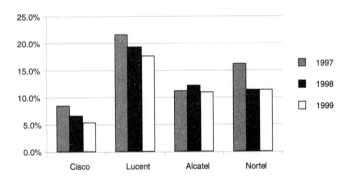

Figure 1.7 PP&E/total assets.

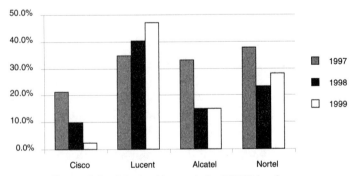

Figure 1.8 (Net working capital + PP&E)/total assets.

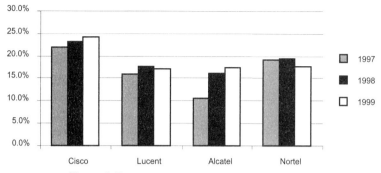

Figure 1.9   R&D/operating costs (COGS, SG&A).

Figure 1.9 suggests the ways in which the available financial capital (as well as human capital) is focused at Cisco. As the chart indicates, a higher proportion of funds flows to research and development, compared with its principal competitors. Figure 1.10 ties these observations together in a chart that captures the degree to which each company in this peer group has adopted a MetaCapitalist approach.

Finally, Figure 1.11 recasts the overall information as a set of summary balance sheet and income statement triangles. The Meta-

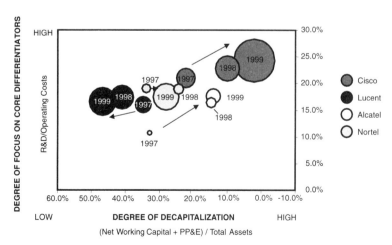

Figure 1.10   Cisco versus competition, 1997–1999.

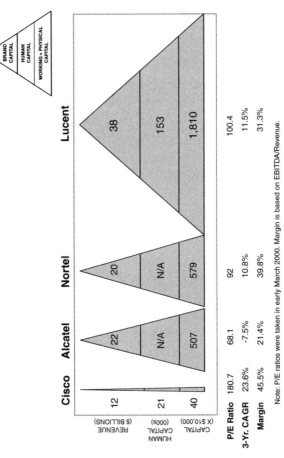

Figure 1.11 Summary balance sheets and income statements.

	Cisco	Alcatel	Nortel	Lucent
REVENUE ($ BILLIONS)	12	22	20	38
HUMAN CAPITAL (000s)	21	N/A	N/A	153
CAPITAL (X $10,000)	40	507	579	1,810
P/E Ratio	180.7	68.1	92	100.4
3-Yr. CAGR	23.6%	-7.5%	10.8%	11.5%
Margin	45.5%	21.4%	39.8%	31.3%

Note: P/E ratios were taken in early March 2000. Margin is based on EBITDA/Revenue.

BRAND CAPITAL
HUMAN CAPITAL
WORKING + PHYSICAL CAPITAL

Capitalist model tends to generate for Cisco a very high P/E ratio: Its multiple is equal to the sum of the same measure for its three largest competitors. On every major performance measure (revenue growth, margin, and margin growth) Cisco leads, with the exception of the margin growth rate of Nortel, which appears to be Cisco's most aggressive competitor in converting to a Meta-Capitalist model. The low P/E ratio for Alcatel appears to be characteristic of companies participating in the Central Europe and Asian markets, which are somewhat more restricted in terms of capital and competition. They are still in the process of transitioning from vertical capital market structures and monopolies, and their overall multiples and performance levels appear to suffer because of these restrictions.

In fairness, we must note that Cisco has built its model without being hampered by a preexisting, large capital base. Companies with large manufacturing operations are traditionally the dominant manufacturer in their sector, produce very impressive results, and represent highly attractive investments. Nonetheless, the discussion does raise the question of how much additional economic growth and value creation will be released as companies adopt the Meta-Capitalist model, outsource much of the manufacturing and related activities that are insufficiently rewarded by the market, and apply an ever larger proportion of their resource base to customer management and product development.

Nortel, for example, has been decapitalizing as well, and to good effect. Last summer, the company announced that it had entered into agreements with five manufacturing firms for the sale and outsourcing of certain facilities. This initiative is part of the company's 18- to 36-month plan to reduce manufacturing and headcount by 8,000 people. To sharpen focus, Nortel recently divested its North American Enterprise Solutions Training business, the Nortel Liberation headset business, and announced that it will more aggressively outsource operations (initially, by $1.5 billion worth of manufacturing in summer 2000). This drive toward a leaner, more focused organization has already increased overall shareholder value: Nortel's market-to-book ratio had grown from the year-end 1999 figure of 11.7 to 16.5 by mid-March 2000, as this book was going to press.

Looking back over this chapter, we will state again that our enormously positive macroeconomic growth projections record our confidence in MetaCapitalism as the best—the inevitable—design for companies and markets in the twenty-first century.

2

The Dynamics of MetaCapitalism: Value-Added Communities and MetaMarkets

In Chapter 1 we discussed the transformation of traditional industrial and financial institutions into decapitalized, brand-owning enterprises with relatively modest physical and working capital. We expect these decapitalized, brand-owning enterprises to focus their financial and human resources on customer ownership and management as well as the management of external alliances and complex outsourced structures such as VACs and MetaMarket networks. All of this will be an enormous change—a revolution.

However, this configuration will allow the brand-owning companies to leverage with outstanding effectiveness their financial, human, and brand capital. It will unleash tremendous new potential for speed and flexibility in responding to market changes and customer requirements. And this, in turn, will create entirely new levels of value in markets served by the new type of enterprise.

Building a direct relationship with the customer, decapitalization, and balance-sheet restructuring will be highly visible manifestations of the B2B revolution and the dramatic new strategies required of companies. These things are, however, only elements in a larger structure: the new MetaCapitalist market. When brand-owning companies redefine themselves, who—to put it bluntly—will make stuff? Who will deliver stuff to customers and handle all the value chain processes that have been outsourced?

The answer lies in the concept of VACs, value-added communities functioning within or evolving into MetaMarkets. As suggested by Figure 2.1, value-added communities may be thought of as networks external to the brand-owning companies. They address supply chain issues involved in producing and delivering product. They supply shared services and related backroom outsourced processes. They provide interfaces along the entire length of the supply and demand chains, including the brand-owning company and its customers. And they supply industry-specific information of all kinds. Sufficient process liquidity is emerging to manage a vari-

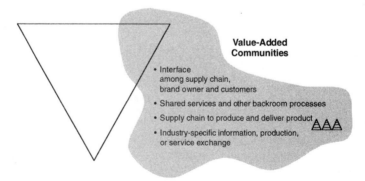

Figure 2.1   Value-added communities.

ety of processes and provide a much finer level of optimization for each element of these business processes. Although it has relinquished many of its processes and functions to one or more external VACs, the brand-owning company can be considered a member of the VAC whether it initiated or controls the overall community. Here is one of the promising singularities of the new design: VACs may organize as such and take the initiative in selecting specific brand-owning companies as alliance partners.

Figure 2.2 charts the process of forming value-added communities. As an industrial company initiates the process of decapitalization and moves to take advantage of the Internet and associated B2B processes and technology (perhaps even of preexisting VACs), it may decapitalize and outsource many traditional functions that formerly existed within its four walls. A significant part or perhaps all of the supply chain may be outsourced, generally into incremental parts. As a first step, for example, the brand-owning company may attempt to organize its existing supply chain partners into a sourcing or delivery network to improve transaction efficiency and lower costs. The alliance agreements governing the new structure will ensure the brand-owning company of sufficient capacity and performance in the outsourced supply chain to deliver the required products and services to its customers.

Similarly, the company may decide to transfer many of its internal management processes—such as financial accounting, human resources, and maintenance, repair, and operations (MRO) procurement—into outsourced networks. These networks may be a captive outsourcing arrangement, supplying services directly to the company through the outsourced units. Or, more likely, they may be a larger "shared services" provider designed to deliver process excellence and scale economies to more than one brand-owning company. Some companies may elect to outsource information technology processes, legal counsel, and elements of marketing and sales, if management regards these functions as non-core to customer management or to the strategic growth drivers of the enterprise. Finally, some processes may be outsourced to industry-specific process managers such as parts and materials market

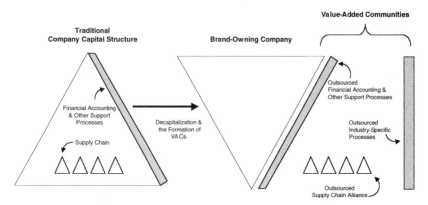

Figure 2.2   The formation of value-added communities.

makers, industry information intermediaries, or transaction special-
ists that provide tailored solutions to sectors such as automotive,
high tech, chemicals, and financial services.

Such value-added communities provide outsourcing options to
companies that wish to decapitalize in order to better leverage their
financial and human resources. But they should also be expected to
function at a much higher performance level than was possible
within the four walls of the brand-owning company. As noted previously, the initiative to form a VAC can come from more than one
source. Suppliers within the supply chain, for example, may form a
VAC to create better markets for themselves.

The key point under any scenario is that the Internet creates
unprecedented opportunities for companies to participate in, and
even create, powerful online trading communities. So doing, they
can achieve the equivalent of continuous, cross-company optimization without direct capital investment. Well-organized VACs, tied
together by orderly process models and technology, will offer
ongoing optimization that easily exceeds the performance levels
the company achieved through wholly owned resources. In short,
lower-capital, brand-owning enterprises can achieve far higher performance than traditional, vertically integrated companies.

Trading communities—value-added communities—will become the great enablers of e-business. Sometimes known as an eMarket, e-commerce hub, infomediary (or MetaMediary), or electronic marketplace, a VAC will enable the optimization of an *entire network* of businesses, in the same way that software advances like ERP have enabled the optimization of *individual* businesses.

VACs create value for participating buyers and suppliers in previously unattainable ways. They revolutionize trading relationships and B2B e-commerce by introducing new efficiencies to the supply chain and new ways of buying and selling products and services. By providing a central platform for transaction automation, information aggregation, improved market liquidity, and extended market reach, they reduce product, process, and sales costs. They leverage more effectively the financial and human resources of decapitalized, brand-owning companies. Further, this is not a zero-sum game; each member of the network comes to the table expecting to leverage the market power, infrastructure, and optimization capability of the VAC. In sum, VACs create powerful benefits for both buyers and sellers: lowered costs of doing business, creation of markets on the network scale, improved service levels.

VACs skillfully leverage the network effect, in the sense that they create buying and selling communities that become more valuable to members as the number of trading partners increases. In the very near future, the potential to increase transaction, sourcing, and market efficiencies will be so high that almost every business will be clamoring to participate. In addition, as discussed in Chapter 4, large networks will begin to exhibit some degree of intelligence through capacities for recognizing patterns, self-organizing behavior, and morphing to more efficient models. They become complex, adaptive systems. Companies that do not join a trading community will be limited by their own infrastructure and market power. They will be as unsuccessful as countries that remain aloof from the world.

VACs form along at least two primary dimensions. As Figure 2.3 indicates, they address either *industry-specific processes* or *cross-industry functional processes*. The former, often referred to as vertical

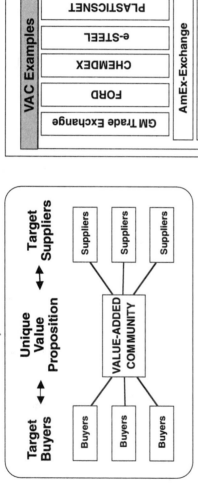

VAC Examples

GM Trade Exchange	FORD	CHEMDEX	e-STEEL	PLASTICSNET

AmEx-Exchange

e.conomy

<u>Vertical Communities</u>
- Resolve industry-specific supply chain inefficiencies

<u>Horizontal Communities</u>
- Cut across industries and automate functional processes such as MRO or logistics

Target Buyers ↔ Unique Value Proposition ↔ Target Suppliers

Buyers		Suppliers
Buyers	VALUE-ADDED COMMUNITY	Suppliers
Buyers		Suppliers

KEY DRIVERS

- Purchasing power
- Process efficiency
- Supply chain integration
- Content/community
- Market efficiency

Figure 2.3 Value–added communities.

communities, are organized by specific industries to resolve specific supply chain inefficiencies (industry "pain points") that lower margins. The latter, or horizontal communities, cut across industries to automate functional processes such as financial accounting, information technology, generic supply chain processes, maintenance, repair and operations (MRO) procurement, and human resource services. In other words, they solve business problems that are common to more than one industry.

Figure 2.4 provides a useful illustration of the dynamics of the value-added community. As the chart suggests, a VAC provides specific support and interaction with the brand-owning company. At the same time, a VAC may continuously change some of the key players within its network to improve operating efficiency or acquire a new competency that will dramatically enhance the processes and performance of the VAC. The dynamics of a VAC are somewhat like the free agency system of the National Basketball Association (NBA) in the United States. Periodically (typically once each year), new players are drafted from new entrants to the league, free agents are picked from a pool of talent within the league, and in some cases players are traded between teams. Similarly, the dynamics of VACs allow new recruits with better products

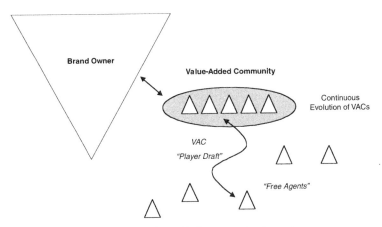

Figure 2.4 Value-added community dynamics.

or processes to replace incumbents. VACs may trade value chain players with players from other VACs that have capabilities that can increase the overall value of the VAC. The point, of course, is to get the right players with the right attributes so that each team can maximize its performance and efficiency at appropriate cost. In the world of VACs, the equivalent of free agency encourages new businesses to enter or replace less effective participants to improve the performance of part or all of the value chain. New entrants gain a special relationship with a brand-owning company as well as with other participants in the VAC. These interfaces are highly dynamic— and they may well evolve toward the larger organization called a MetaMarket.

As Figure 2.5 suggests, some of the free agents joining a VAC may be selected not only because of their own capabilities, but also because of alliances they have created elsewhere. These alliances may allow them to bring to the VAC options such as reserve manufacturing capacity or perhaps specialized process or technology skills. In any case, the VAC begins to create competition at what we have called the molecular level. This promotes an ever-increasing optimization typically unattainable when supply chains are largely controlled within the four walls of individual companies. Thus, VACs can provide tremendous leverage for financial and human capital.

At the highest level, VACs draw their strength from three key characteristics:

- Buyers and suppliers can connect to each other through VACs with relative ease.

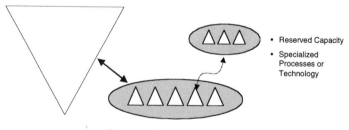

Figure 2.5 Options players.

- With the participation of numerous buyers and suppliers, market liquidity is created on both the supply side (cost and quality) and the demand side (market scale).
- They are actively managed—they are the business of a team of businesses—and the network becomes an important, perhaps the *most important* business in each sector.

Despite their seeming simplicity, creating and maintaining a VAC is far from simple. Brand-owning companies may manage the VAC or simply participate. Varied and first-rate skills are required initially to define the value proposition for the community. The systems infrastructure challenge is massive. And assuming a good start, a VAC must be actively managed to sustain both the community and the value created. The need for active, expert management has led to the rise of online intermediaries known as *eMarketMakers.* Those who play this role must combine a deep understanding of industry dynamics, market players, and power balances with the ability to design and deliver a sustainable value proposition. They must earn and retain the trust of both suppliers and buyers. In addition, eMarketMakers require sufficient resources and technology expertise to create a common platform for managing digital trade across multiple electronic standards (e.g., XML). Finally, developing and sustaining a VAC requires the ability to create a new operating model to derive all the benefits previously outlined.

Perhaps the clearest way to conceptualize a VAC is as a unique value proposition that links target buyers and target suppliers. The following seven levers, separately or in combination, create the value proposition of virtually any VAC:

- **Purchasing power.** A VAC derives its purchasing power value from aggregating demand in a buying consortium. This results in such benefits as volume pricing, sophisticated information for supplier negotiations, consolidation of suppliers, and spending and control reports.
- **Process efficiency and operational excellence.** Integrating sourcing, purchasing, billing, and payment vastly

reduces the cost of acquisition for goods, services, and customers. VACs that offer process efficiency must build functionality, including electronic requisition and approval, improved and continuous financial accounting and reporting, better sales and customer management, and improved information access—all of which reduces transaction and work-flow costs. VACs may provide additional value to members by achieving operational excellence in the management of select procurement and processes, including strategic sourcing and spend monitoring and control.

- **Supply chain integration.** The value proposition in this area might include disintermediation, reintermediation, improved visibility across market supply chains, reduced lead time, reduced inventory levels, improved logistics management, and ERP-related process integration.
- **Aggregated content/community.** This lever includes the value gained from knowledge brought to the network, be it industry best practices, knowledge management, benchmarking studies, or other content-based value. Categories include monitoring and control reports, discussion forums, product information and reviews, frequently asked questions (FAQs), and newsletters.
- **Market efficiency.** VACs offering this value proposition provide online market-making mechanisms (e.g., e-Catalog, auctions, exchanges, and bid processes) that match buyers and suppliers to improve both market and product liquidity and remove search time from the buying and selling process. By creating a marketplace of aggregated buyers and sellers, the VAC provides members with broader access, improved market knowledge, and new sales opportunities for both buyers and sellers.
- **Accelerated market growth and customer control.** By leveraging financial and human capital, as well as Internet channels to the customer, brand-owning VAC participants can dramatically expand market reach and responsiveness to their customers.

- **Collaboration.** Members of the VAC can utilize its relative transparency to plan jointly, for example, production planning and capacity management or performance review and improvement.

Figure 2.6 summarizes these value propositions.

The applicability and importance of each value category is a function of the relevant industry, process efficiencies and inefficiencies, targeted community, size of the target buyer, and type of goods or services purchased (e.g., commodity, near commodity, or custom engineered).

We expect VACs to continue their evolution along these key dimensions, further enhancing their value to participating members. In addition, eMarketMakers will augment the offering with other service differentiators that may include payment processing, risk management, escrow and financial settlements, back-end integration, and expediting import/export. VACs will soon resemble electronic *keiretsus*.

The important principle in Figure 2.7 is that the trend will evolve from optimization of an *individual* business to optimization of a *network* of businesses. Presently, many companies are using the power of e-business to optimize their individual supply chains and sales/distribution processes. Much of the online B2B trade to date has focused on improving transaction and workflow inefficiencies—in other words, moving purchasing and selling from conventional channels to the Internet.

Although implementing e-procurement software or creating online storefronts may allow a company to manage its supplier relationships more effectively and/or decrease its cost of sales, these approaches inevitably require significant up-front investments by a single seller or buyer. As a result, such solutions are structurally inefficient and fundamentally limited.

Similarly, companies that employ current technology platforms like electronic data interchange (EDI) or extranets to optimize a network of trading partners have parted with significant dollars to realize the benefits of network optimization. For most companies,

Value Levers

Aggregated Content/ Community	Market Efficiency	Process Efficiency	Purchase Power	Supply Chain Integration	Accelerated Market Growth	Collaboration

• Industry best practices
• Industry news, associations, references
• Benchmarking studies
• Monitoring/Control reports
• Discussion forums
• Product information and reviews
• FAQs
• Industry collaboration
• Career services
• Newsletters
• Network effect
	• Online market-making mechanisms to match buyers and suppliers
	  – e-Catalog
	  – Auctions
	  – Exchanges
	  – Bid processes
	• Access to broader range of suppliers and buyers
	• Improved Information access
		• Electronic order taking and management
		• Electronic requisition and approval (work flow)
		• Auto replenishment
		• Electronic bill presentment/ payment
		• Improved information access
		• Better spend control
		• Electronic targeted marketing collateral and promotions
		• Reduced transaction costs
			• Aggregate buyers into buying consortiums
			• Volume pricing
			• Better information for supplier negotiations
			• Supplier consolidation
			• Spending and control reports
				• Disintermediation
				• Improved visibility across market supply chains
				• Reduced lead time
				• Reduced inventory levels
				• Improved logistics management
				• ERP integration
					• Leverage financial & human capital
					• Concentrate on customer acquisition & management
					• Leverage Internet channels— greatly expand accessible markets
						• Decision support
						• Production planning
						• Capacity management

Figure 2.6 VACs create value for their members through a combination of seven levers.

ENTERPRISE OPTIMIZATION

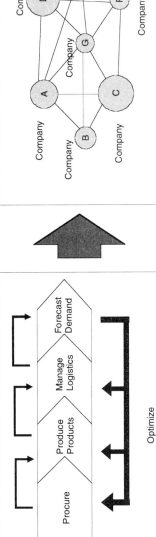

Optimize

- ☑ Independently manages hundreds of supplier relationships
- ☑ Limited to its own market power and infrastructure
- ☑ Customer and market access limited by front office organizational capacity
- ☑ Optimizes its own supply chain
- ☑ Procurement through manual or semiautomated processes

NETWORK OPTIMIZATION

Company Company Company Company Company Company Company Company Company

(A, B, C, D, E, F, G network diagram)

- ☑ Communities of similar businesses jointly manage suppliers
- ☑ Leverage the market power and infrastructure of many
- ☑ Access customers through established networks
- ☑ Optimize a market supply chain vs. an individual supply chain
- ☑ Automated end-to-end e-procurement solutions (requisition to payment)
- ☑ Leverage financial, human, and brand capital and focus on market

Figure 2.7 E-business is driving a fundamental transformation in B2B commerce—shifting from optimizing an individual business to optimizing a network of businesses for competitive advantage.

the cost of participating in these networks or trading communities ultimately outstrips the benefits. And for those companies that do participate, the costly investments (and significant configuration associated with EDI) severely limit the numbers of trading partners with which any company can connect. The result?—an inflexible solution that restricts competition and is subject to artificial market barriers.

Although the VAC business model is just beginning to take shape, a number of VACs have already begun to form and that number is expected to grow dramatically in the next few years. Examples of emerging VACs include VerticalNet, Chemdex, and Bizzed.com, each of which either targets specific industry groups or solves a functional need. These early-stage VACs typically focus on only one or two of the value levers, and they often target small to midsize businesses. Many are developing as content or community portals (e.g., VerticalNet, Bizzed.com), in this respect replicating the business-to-consumer model of using community to drive commerce. Other VACs leverage enabling technologies to create market and process efficiencies through bids, auctions (TradeOut), exchanges (ChemConnect), or catalog aggregation (Chemdex). As the market matures, eMarketMakers must continue to enhance their value propositions to remain competitive: They must engage more value levers to develop increasingly sophisticated B2B solutions. One of the key strategic issues for a VAC is how to hold together in the face of growing competition. Some will try to create significant switching costs through technology, process protocols, and services, as well as by adding value levers.

The MetaMarket

The VAC is an extraordinary innovation. Yet a still newer and larger market-shaping entity is expected to arise by mid-2000 (see Figure 2.8). Known as MetaMarkets, these nascent forces will consist of portfolios of VACs joined together to bring even greater levels of value to the online business system. First and foremost,

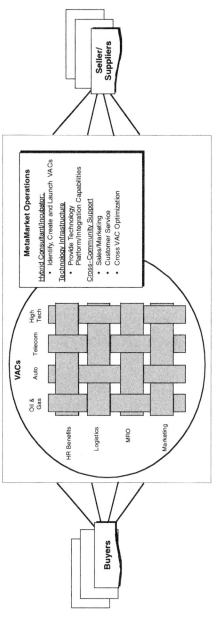

DRIVERS

- Speed: ability to rapidly form and launch VACs
- Scale: operational efficiencies across community shared services
- Synergy: expanded community and collaboration opportunities

Figure 2.8 The MetaMarket: a portfolio of VACs.

MetaMarkets will provide buyers with convenient portals to make contact with the vast spectrum of purchasing.

MetaMarkets will establish portfolios of VACs, built on a common technology platform, to provide members a cost-effective and comprehensive offering of products and services. In this way, Meta-Markets will seek to build and maintain a critical mass of buyers and sellers. Leveraging the benefits of economies of scale, Meta-Market providers will rapidly develop new VACs on an ongoing basis to complement their offerings for existing members. This continuous process of VAC formation will draw on the established customer base as well as the underlying technology platform and back-office shared services of the MetaMarket (e.g., billing, customer service).

Figure 2.9 depicts the dynamic nature of MetaMarkets. As the figure suggests, the MetaMarket knits together a set of VACs (in this case, VAC-1 and VAC-2) to provide an integrated suite of service offerings to customers in support of the brand-owning company. The MetaMarket has a set of process protocols and technologies that glue it together, connecting the VACs with one another and with the brand-owning company. In addition, scale and network effects raise switching costs to hold VACs together and maintain the coherence of the MetaMarket. Continuous optimization allows the VACs to improve their processes at the sub-VAC or individual business level, either through successful internal efforts or by trading out current participants in the VAC for new participants capable of supporting a higher level of optimization and performance. As the figure illustrates, this process of optimization and replacement can occur not only at the VAC level but also at the MetaMarket level. The MetaMarket may trade one VAC (VAC-1) for an entirely different VAC (VAC-3) if management believes that this will enhance the overall performance of the MetaMarket. In addition, MetaMarkets compete against each other to develop the best process, technology, and management models and ultimately to create the best integrated suite of businesses from the perspective of customers and consumers.

Independent VACs, meanwhile, will be forced to join a Meta-Market or risk being competitively overwhelmed by MetaMarkets,

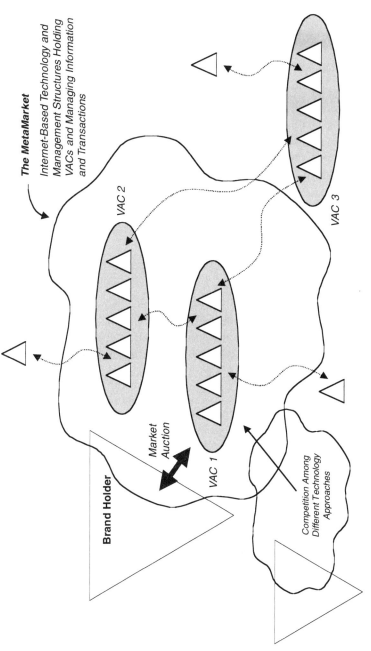

Figure 2.9 Continuous restructuring and competition among VACs—the formation of a MetaMarket suite of VACs.

which can be expected to leverage their economies of scale and sprout new VACs. Both buyers and suppliers will benefit from membership in a MetaMarket, owing to their greater reach, breadth of offerings, and opportunities for collaboration. These strong network effects and the economies of scale inherent in MetaMarkets will drive many industries to become true oligopolies, dominated by a few global players. The ultimate winners can be expected to emerge over the next few years. There is tremendous advantage for those who move quickly and decisively now to solidify their market positions through strategic partnerships, acquisitions, and joint ventures—the molecular biology of VACs and MetaMarkets.

Like VACs, MetaMarkets will require active, expert management to drive industry transformation and convergence through the cross-optimization of VACs. Only those MetaMarket providers that bring certain core competencies to the table will be able to stake significant claims to this opportunity. Such providers will need a deep understanding of multiple industry-specific supply chains to rapidly develop comprehensive portfolios of horizontal and vertical VACs. In addition, MetaMarkets will need access to broad communities of buyers and sellers to gain the competitive advantage of critical mass. The differentiating competence of a MetaMarket will rest on its ability to develop and integrate for the community a technology platform that makes VACs interoperable on the front end while integrating them into buyer and seller systems on the back end.

Currently, no single entity is strongly positioned to provide this full range of capabilities. The likely scenario is that a community of partners, leveraging their collective synergies, will create MetaMarkets. Here again there is a restriction: Probably only a few players currently possess the size, power, and breadth and depth of experience to enroll in such a community of providers. Those best positioned are leading companies in their industries, capable of rapidly decapitalizing and becoming brand-owning companies as well as MetaMarket managers. Suitable candidates may also be external service providers with deep industry knowledge, reputations for extreme trustworthiness, large customer bases on which to draw in building the communities, and the necessary information technology (IT) capability. Such service providers are likely to partner with large IT vendors and/or software vendors whose strengths include enabling technologies and market visibility. Finally, with their unmatched ability to acquire and develop new customer relationships, financial institutions have the potential to emerge as key contributors to the formation of MetaMarkets.

Success like that of VACs will rely largely on the ability to develop a community of providers, based on mutually established need, to leverage the power of many. Needless to say, businesses participating in MetaMarkets and value-added communities need to be extremely dynamic and to work continuously to improve their performance.

From a strategic perspective, each of these players—brand-owning companies, companies participating in VACs, companies wishing to participate in VACs, managers of VACs, and MetaMarket managers—will need to incorporate a strategic process resembling the continuous asset transformation engine (CATE). The CATE (Figure 2.10) is a strategic process in which the business considers ways to engage in dramatic improvement either in its own contributions to the value chain or in its interfaces with other members of a VAC or MetaMarket. The CATE discipline requires a company's leaders to look for internal process or performance improvements as well as to search continuously for alliances that will create more value for the enterprise. Leading players in Meta-

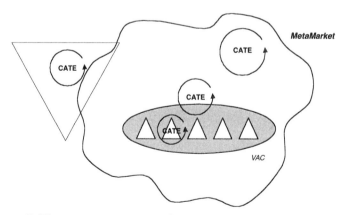

Figure 2.10 Continuous asset transformation engines (CATEs) keeping up with the optimization of MetaCapitalism.

Capitalism report that they have reduced their strategic planning cycle from five years to three years to one year to three months to one day. This is the level of intensity displayed by successful companies such as Cisco and Microsoft.

Not only strategic planning, but many other internal processes within such companies display unprecedented efficiency. For example, leading players currently practice continuous financial accounting. They have the capacity to close their books daily. The benefits are numerous: They can create alliances and drive deals without delay, and they have access to numbers that genuinely support the CATE. All of this is a persuasive sign that the competence and speed of the management teams of major institutions are dramatically increasing.

The message is clear. In the New Economy, *the network will be the business.* The advent of value-added communities, aggregated and managed through MetaMarkets, is too important to ignore. Ultimately, these entities will survive and prosper through their ability to win and keep members. At the speed these forces are taking shape, early adopters will be richly rewarded and latecomers severely penalized. With traditional sales and distribution channels crumbling around us, the stakes are nothing less than survival.

To conclude this discussion of VACs and MetaMarkets, we want to call attention to these associated concepts:

- **The continuous morphing of MetaMarkets.** As Figure 2.11 indicates, the dynamism of MetaMarkets leads to a cycle of continuous birth and rebirth. The chart suggests that as a MetaMarket becomes successful it may achieve a brand identity of its own. Because this new or essentially new brand is supported by

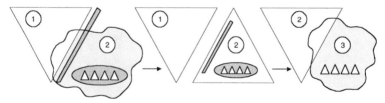

Figure 2.11 Morphing of a MetaMarket into a brand holder and back to a MetaMarket.

large process and supply chain structures, the MetaMarket may evolve into an enterprise with a broad capital base and direct customer contacts—much like the large, highly capitalized industrial companies that dominated the twentieth century. However, the MetaCapitalist operating patterns we have been exploring in this chapter may persuade the management of such a MetaMarket to disintermediate and align with a new MetaMarket to succeed. If the new MetaMarket turns out to be more successful than the old at customer acquisition and channel control, the brand-owning companies in the old MetaMarket may need to align with new MetaMarkets or disappear entirely. Such is the cycle of intense competition and realignment produced by MetaCapitalism. The dynamism of MetaMarkets is more fully discussed in Chapter 4.

- **Sunk costs.** MetaCapitalism is low on sentimentality and relatively high on anonymity. When it works well, nearly any enterprise can attempt to achieve a level of performance and optimization that will allow it to participate in a value-added community. Similarly, new technologies that provide the integrating "glue" for MetaMarkets may be overtaken by even better technologies. As a part of their CATE, all players in a MetaMarket need to consider continuously whether it's time to move on to a new VAC or MetaMarket, and whether the time has come to trade out or upgrade technology or other infrastructure. Institutions will need to take a much harder line on recognizing sunk costs and moving on to new approaches. The business analysis for these transitions will be captured in options theory analysis (see Chapter 6). Creating value and sustaining economic growth in the new world of MetaCapitalism will be, at times, a harsh process. On the other hand, failure to create value and remain competitive will be much harsher.

- **Transparency.** For companies to succeed in the environment of VACs and MetaMarkets, they must be transparent in certain respects. Alliance partners throughout a MetaMarket will need a clear understanding of the supply chain and business process architecture of their partners. As we observed earlier, to be able to make large alliances and deals quickly, companies will need processes for continuous financial accounting and reporting. They will need the capacity to close their books daily and to report their financial position at any moment—either fully audited or with sufficient assurance to be useful in market transactions. These requirements suggest an entirely new level of process efficiency and management discipline. Companies will need to dramatically improve internal performance analysis and decision-making infrastructures so that transparency is a strategic advantage rather than a costly burden.

■ **Internal e-processes.** In addition to having a CATE and transparent processes, successful participants in a MetaMarket must manage most of their internal business processes on the Internet. By using the Internet for human resources, financial accounting, R&D, operations management, marketing, and so on, companies will enhance their speed, efficiency, and transparency. Some of the most successful New Economy enterprises, as well as major companies going through the transformation to e-business, have made clear that their key management processes must all be network-based.

■ **Shifting locus of MetaMarket management.** As Figure 2.12 suggests, the locus of management of VACs and MetaMarkets can be centered in the brand-owning company, in the supply base, in a balance between the two, in a balanced system managed from the outside (possibly by a trusted third party), or in an integrated supply chain manager (either a player in the MetaMarket or a trusted third party). Because the dynamics of each MetaMarket are different, strategic analysis must consider where the most effective locus of power is likely to be centered.

■ **Inevitability.** Figure 2.13 suggests how maintaining a large company based on physical capital creates so many types of value drains that, in future, such structures are unlikely to succeed in any industry. We believe that MetaMarkets will prevail in nearly every sector in response to this value drain.

A Word—and a Chart—on the Ancestry of MetaCapitalism

These trends do not emerge exclusively from the advent of new technologies. They build on the major business and economic trans-

VAC Models

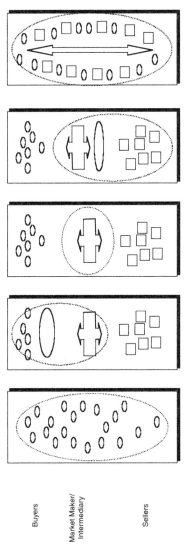

Buyers

Market Maker/
Intermediary

Sellers

Model Type	Eco-System	Community of Mutual Interest (Buyer Led)	Neutral Exchange (1)	Distributor (Seller Led)	Integrated Supply Chain
Example	GM-Commerce One	e.conomy	e-steel	Grainger.com	Rosetta Net (2)
Characteristics	All suppliers to GM are linked with GM and, where applicable, each other	Groups of buyers with common needs/interests align to gain leverage (can be with or without anchor tenant)	Community forms around common exchange of buyers and sellers (no dominant party necessarily)	Distributors group sellers to focus on a common group of buyers	Neutral party builds platform for e-business within a vertical market (e.g., high technology)

(1) can be initiated by dominant players on the sell or buy side or neutral parties (e.g., free markets)
(2) under development

Figure 2.12 VACs will develop around different models.

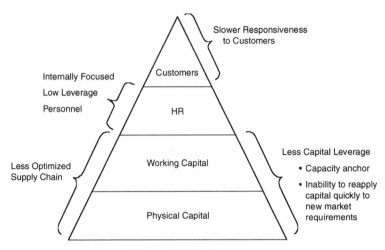

Figure 2.13 Value Drain.

formations that have occurred over the past 20 years. In our book, *Wisdom of the CEO,* we traced the pattern of change in the past 20 years and indicated how this led directly to the business issues facing major companies as the new century approached. Unless companies have adopted many of the valid management practices, processes, and technologies gained during those two decades of change, they will not be equipped to participate in VACs or MetaMarkets. Companies must have found a fruitful relation with globally integrated capital markets. They must have achieved some real degree of supply chain synchronization and sound ERP process standards. They must have forged a new understanding of core competency. If all this has not come to pass, they will face Clayton Christensen's "innovator's dilemma"—they will lack the requisite platforms and skills to make the transition to decapitalized brand-owning companies, participating with high efficiency in MetaMarkets.

Figure 2.14 provides a partial ancestry of MetaCapitalism and the key events of the past 20 years that set the stage for the B2B e-business revolution.

The flow from left to right in this chart invites a number of observations:

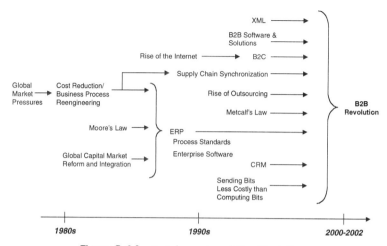

Figure 2.14   Partial ancestry of MetaCapitalism.

- The global market pressures of the 1980s led to aggressive cost-reduction initiatives, often packaged as business process reengineering. These initiatives set the stage for supply chain synchronization and process standardization through ERP, which yielded the highly flexible, low cycle time, standard process models required for MetaMarket optimization. While these transitions can perhaps never be completed in every sense of the word, there has been much progress. If the VAC and MetaMarket models had occurred before these transitions, outsourcing would have "hardwired" inflexible processes based on economies of scale—the opposite of what is needed to achieve continuous optimization leveraging the Internet.

- As companies moved during the late 1980s and early 1990s to create a global operations infrastructure, they set the stage for addressing a broad and growing global market. Global marketing, branding, supply chain and financial processes, and human resources and management processes are needed for B2B and B2C e-businesses to take advantage of their new options and increasingly accessible markets. If companies have not fully evaluated their external and internal processes from the perspective of global requirements, their potential for success and rapid growth will be severely limited.

- The rapid expansion of ERP systems in the 1990s, based on the economics of Moore's law, created a vast IT infrastructure as well as a good understanding and acceptance of enterprise systems. These gains have favored a smooth transition to the technology systems that support MetaMarkets.

- Similarly, the application of Moore's law in the 1990s, accelerated greatly by the Internet, created conditions at the turn of the century in which the cost of moving bits dropped below that of computing bits, thus leading to the network-based solutions underpinning the B2B revolution.

- The business process transformations of the early 1990s, combined with an increased focus on core competencies, led to a dramatic rise in the outsourcing of business processes— again, a preparation for MetaMarkets.

- Finally, the rise and growing use of the Internet, the surge of B2C businesses, and the adoption of standardized languages such as XML, provided the framework necessary for B2B e-business.

In short, the business-to-business-to-consumer (B2B2C) revolution is not just an overnight phenomenon tied to a new technology. It is the sum and extension of a series of trends that have been building for 20 years.

Earlier we proposed this equation:

$$e_{(business\text{-}to\text{-}business)} = M \ (Change \times Courage)$$

We hope that its meaning is now clearer. The complexity and pressures attendant on the change to MetaCapitalism are enormous. But the rewards and satisfaction of doing business in the new configuration will be greater than ever for those who have the courage to begin soon, very soon, and to persevere.

3 | New Business Process Models for B2B

Business process models will change as major companies make the transition to the MetaMarket world. Traditionally (see Figure 3.1), the model for a manufacturing company might include sourcing, manufacturing, distribution, and sales, typically integrated into a synchronized supply chain owned and operated for the most part by the company itself. Closely aligned with the supply chain would be product development, marketing, and promotion processes. Financial, IT, and communications systems would support these core business processes. While this traditional process model, like the MetaMarket models to be outlined in this chapter, derives from the manufacturing sector, the basic concepts apply equally well to other sectors such as financial services, regulated businesses, and even public or governmental institutions. We will look at some of those applications in Chapter 5.

During the 1980s and early 1990s, process models in most companies focused on incremental process reengineering, in the course of which process maps were designed for individual companies and non-value-added steps were removed or replaced with more value-adding activities (see Figure 3.2). For many sectors this involved the development of "just-in-time" (JIT) processes, in which demand

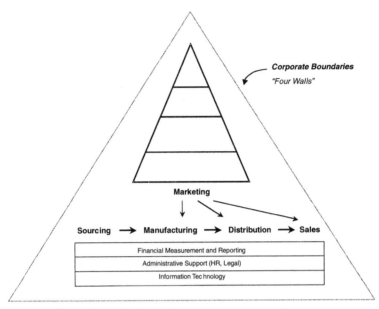

Figure 3.1   Traditional business processes/manufacturing.

signals trigger quick and flexible responses to manufacture and ship parts or services to the next step in the process chain. The elimination of non-value-added steps, achievement of cycle time reductions, and implementation of just-in-time approaches conferred an enormous advantage. By adopting a time-based approach to process design, inventory was reduced throughout the enterprise, working capital efficiency improved dramatically, and overall market responsiveness improved as well. On the other hand, these improved processes were still plagued with significant working capital problems such as inventory spikes, bottlenecks and shortages, and the need for excess reserve capacity in the event that demand increased unpredictably and the lean reserves of inventory and production capacity proved inadequate to meet that demand. While excess inventory and inefficient use of working capital were targeted as serious problems during this period, an even more serious problem was the inability to fill orders.

During this phase of supply chain and process improvement,

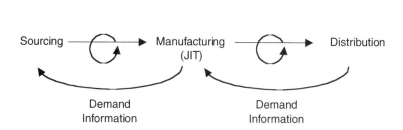

Problems

- Inventory Spikes
- Bottlenecks/Shortages
- Excess Reserved Capacity
- Moderate Improvements in Customer Responsiveness

Figure 3.2 Isolated supply chain improvement.

there were many instances of premature outsourcing and process automation. The use of EDI to better connect elements of the supply chain, or the installation of automated manufacturing technology, often tended to exacerbate supply chain misalignments rather than improve them. Where cycle time was reduced in one part of a process but fed into processes where there were significant bottlenecks, work in process inventory would often spike and thus cause significant working capital charges. Installation of EDI or automation in this type of process flow could lead to even larger inventory spikes. Outsourcing the processes tended to hardwire the problems and made them even more difficult to correct through further process reengineering. Figure 3.3 provides a high-level schematic for this type of premature outsourcing and automation.

If Internet-based, MetaMarket solutions had been applied to process models during this period, that approach would have further exacerbated the inefficiencies. The result would not have been a dynamic and continuously improving MetaMarket, but rather an

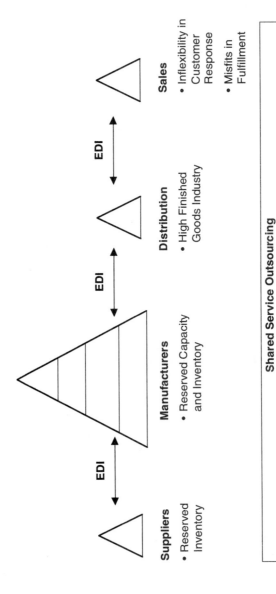

Suppliers
- Reserved Inventory

Manufacturers
- Reserved Capacity and Inventory

Distribution
- High Finished Goods Industry

Sales
- Inflexibility in Customer Response
- Misfits in Fulfillment

EDI

Shared Service Outsourcing

Hardwired misalignment with customer needs

Figure 3.3 Premature outsourcing and EDI: automating the "as-is" rather than the "to be."

automated, suboptimally performing supply chain easily whip-sawed by fluctuations in demand and subject to erratic responses.

During the 1990s, most companies continued to evolve their business process models in the direction of synchronized supply chains. The key to success was to share market and demand information smoothly throughout the supply chain. This practice reduced end-to-end cycle time and dramatically dampened inventory spikes and working capital requirements. Synchronized supply chains led to balanced capacity planning and usage and enormous improvements in customer responsiveness. At the same time, ERP systems tended somewhat to standardize best practice models and provided technology products to better enable and manage these improved process models within the four walls of the institution. Figure 3.4 provides an overview of the synchronized supply chain model and its benefits.

At the same time that supply chains were being improved, marketing and synchronized demand chains were taking advantage of these process advances. Now that brand and promotional strategies

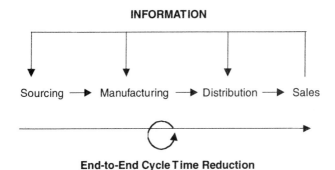

INFORMATION

Sourcing ⟶ Manufacturing ⟶ Distribution ⟶ Sales

End-to-End Cycle Time Reduction

- Balanced Capacity Planning and Usage
- Reduced Inventory Spikes and Working Capital Requirements
- Enormous Improvements in Customer Responsiveness
- Somewhat ERP-Enabled within Four Walls

Figure 3.4 Synchronized supply chain.

could be based on highly responsive supply chains, marketing managers were able to dramatically lower product development and promotional cycle times, support synchronized capacity planning, and confidently attack new markets. They knew that the supply chain would allow the company to scale up marketing initiatives quickly and capitalize on unexpected market opportunities. Increasingly, Customer Relationship Management (CRM) systems began to standardize these processes and interface closely with ERP systems in support of these process advances. Figure 3.5 summarizes the demand chain improvements as they were aligned with the supply chain.

Figure 3.6 brings these concepts together to suggest the overall evolution of processes during the past 15 to 20 years. A model based on traditional economies of scale, with episodic efficiency improvements, evolves into a synchronized supply and demand chain process model enhanced by ERP and CRM systems. It then encounters the B2B revolution, in which outsourced processes are regrouped into VACs and dynamic MetaMarkets.

The process models of efficient VACs and MetaMarkets build systematically from prior configurations to new process concepts and improvements. Absent this relatively long sequential evolution of business process thinking, the Internet seed might have fallen on barren ground. It would not today promise the accelerated wealth

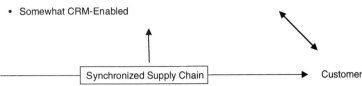

Marketing

- Rapid Product Development and Promotion Cycle
- Rapid Brand Response to Market
- Synchronized Capacity Planning
- Capability to Efficiently Scale Up on a Domestic or Global Basis
- Somewhat CRM-Enabled

Synchronized Supply Chain ⟶ Customer

Figure 3.5 Synchronized demand chain and marketing.

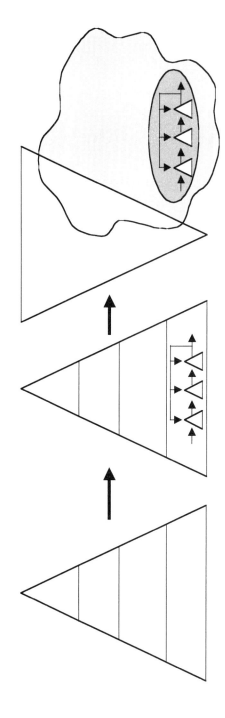

Traditional Company
Managed Economies of
Scale and Episodic
Efficiency

Synchronized
Supply & Demand Chain
Processes with ERP/CRM

Decapitalized/Outsourced
Company

Figure 3.6   Process evolution to MetaMarkets.

and growth potential that we confidently anticipate over the next few years.

Figure 3.7 outlines the key characteristics required of processes in the B2B environment. The new process model must

- Be able to operate seamlessly across the VAC/MetaMarket network.
- Be able to operate with the speed and efficiency of the synchronized supply chain and continuously improve performance.
- Allow for VAC players to opt in and opt out to improve the overall performance of the VAC.
- Be able to serve multiple channels along the supply chain from the brand-owning company to customers, who have direct access to the supply chain owing to the disintermediation that has occurred.
- Provide sufficient flexibility and transparency for self-service so that customers, business partners, and employees can actively affect the performance and activities of the VAC to continuously optimize performance.
- Perform as a synchronized supply chain so that the processes support one-to-one customer service, that is, high-speed, mass customization.
- Allow demand, capacity, and price to be optimized so that the model pulls product through the supply chain to support mass customization. It must also pull planning and capacity allocation, and support an auction capability so that excess product or capacity can be pushed at efficient prices through the network.

For illustrative purposes, Figure 3.8 provides an overview of a generic MetaMarket process model. As the figure suggests, conventional processes have been replaced by new types of processes reflecting the dynamic nature of VACs and the MetaMarket.

One key process is the ability to manage the business concept life cycle. Network players will need to be extremely facile in

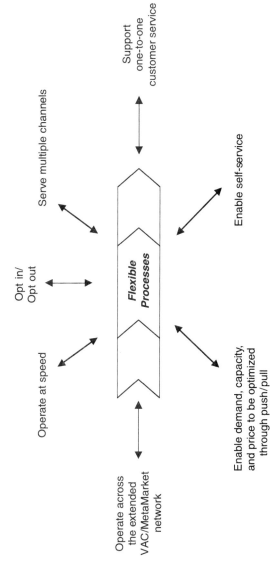

Figure 3.7 B2B process design characteristics.

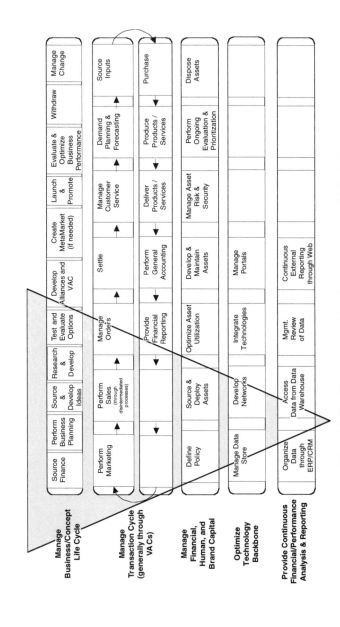

Figure 3.8 Illustrative example of a new process model for B2B.

rapidly identifying new business concepts, creating appropriate alliances and forming VACs and MetaMarkets, managing these businesses, and winding down or transforming the businesses as they reach the end of their life cycle. As with all aspects of business in the next few years, change will come fast, and life cycles will be shorter—necessitating a dynamic business management process.

Similarly, there is a need to manage the transaction cycles within VACs and the overall MetaMarkets. Entirely new management competencies will be required to control transactions in an outsourced, integrated network. If handled effectively, transaction costs should drop dramatically, and flexibility and speed should improve substantially. The principles of management and management leverage as well as communications processes and technologies will be significantly different than if the processes were within the four walls of the company.

One of the key features of the MetaMarket model is the potential to manage financial, human, and brand capital more effectively and leverage them across a broader market. Processes that carefully examine capital leverage, assess the core leverage points for value creation, and concentrate the business on growth and performance improvement will again differ dramatically from conventional approaches.

Just as members of the supply chain VAC will change continuously, so too will the technology backbone. New technology approaches and players will emerge continuously, requiring the need for internal processes to manage these technology transitions and improvements. Finally, the VAC will require financial and transactional transparency both to support transactions and to drive market value. Continuous financial and performance analysis and reporting will become the norm—and represent a significant qualitative improvement in financial processes.

All of these processes require tremendous discipline and management capability. They allow companies to leverage capital and create value quickly. But they pressure management to be insightful, decisive, and flexible.

While supply chain issues remain important, they will be

increasingly the responsibility of VACs and MetaMarkets, rather than of individual enterprises. VACs and MetaMarkets focus on optimizing the supply chain—this is their core competency. They are less involved in product development and brand management. For the brand-owning company linked into a MetaMarket, key concerns are alliance development and outsourcing management. Rapid alliance development is a core competency: The company must be able to take newly designed products or services and rapidly create alliances to manufacture those products or provide those services to the marketplace. The ingredients are highly skilled financial accounting, very rapid M&A decision making, insightful negotiation, and efficient deal transaction processing. In addition, the ability to design and implement outsourced networks rapidly is essential in this style of market. Continuous monitoring and management of the outsourced network must also be counted as a key competency. While not directly responsible for the manufacture and delivery of products, the brand-owning company needs sufficient controls and systems to assure that its alliance partners are well integrated with each other and the marketplace and perform at the levels of speed, quality, and cost required by the marketplace.

An additional set of key processes is customer understanding, customer management, and customer channel control. The focus of the brand-owning company is on customers—to understand their requirements and needs and to design and launch products and services that meet those needs. Much of the communication to gather information and market products and services takes place over the Internet. This new pattern suggests a dramatically sharpened focus on product development and R&D (both "e" based), combined with tremendous expansion of the resources and attention given to customer understanding and responsiveness.

Figure 3.9 provides a taxonomy of suggested process models for the various business participants in a MetaMarket and outlines a series of processes common to all players within it. Because of the high level of disintermediation in MetaMarkets, there are many types of participating businesses, each with distinct processes enabling its specific role in the MetaMarket. We used the term *molecular* previously to refer to this level of VACs and MetaMarkets. At this molecular level, the participating enterprises' focus on their own roles and processes generates the economic liquidity of MetaMarkets and encourages the continuous optimization of each player.

As noted earlier, processes for the brand-owning companies tend to focus on consumer and customer management as well as alliance development and management. (These processes are also suggested in Figure 3.8.) The processes for the brand-owning company contrast with those of VAC supply chain participants. These businesses focus on continuous improvements in the efficiency of their contribution to the supply chain, in keeping with the overall structure and objectives of the synchronized VAC supply chain in which they participate.

Shared services businesses use economies of scale and process excellence to deliver specific, high-quality services (e.g., human resources (HR), financial accounting, IT support, legal, and perhaps some generic version of marketing and sales). The technology developers and implementers that provide the glue for VACs and MetaMarkets are similar to shared service providers in their focus on delivering highest-quality solutions to their broad range of customers.

Business processes for VAC managers and MetaMarket managers tend to focus on the organization and management of the overall network as well as management of their transactional and information x-change (infomediary) activities. Because their success derives from the performance levels achieved by the VAC or MetaMarket, carefully monitoring end-to-end performance, managing transactions, exchanging information, and troubleshooting are their primary processes. Earlier, we described VACs and Meta-Markets as building and rebuilding their teams under something resembling the NBA free agent system. Within this analogy, VAC managers behave like the general managers of individual teams and MetaMarket managers are the organizers and managers of the overall league.

Of course, MetaMarkets are bound together by a series of

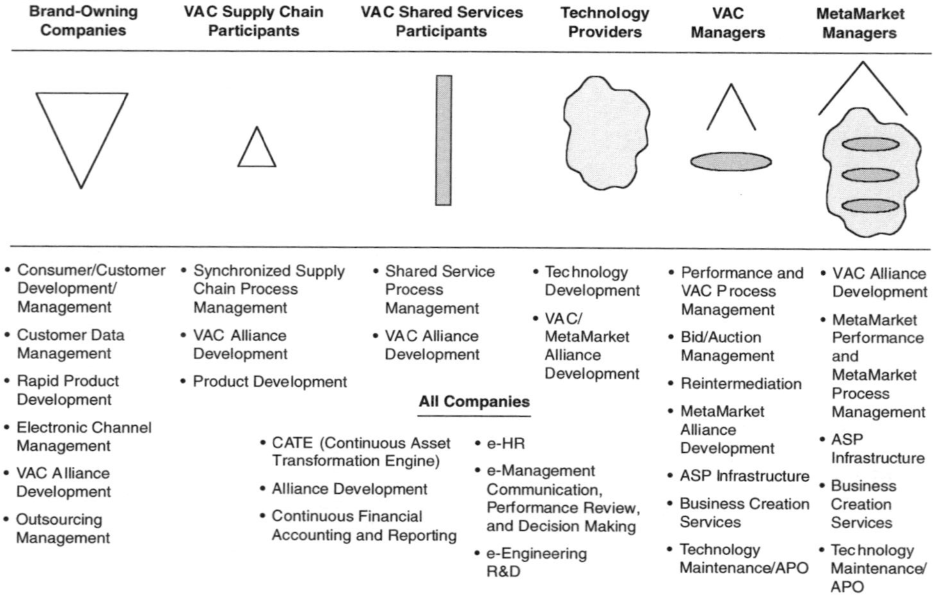

Brand-Owning Companies	VAC Supply Chain Participants	VAC Shared Services Participants	Technology Providers	VAC Managers	MetaMarket Managers

- Consumer/Customer Development/Management
- Customer Data Management
- Rapid Product Development
- Electronic Channel Management
- VAC Alliance Development
- Outsourcing Management

- Synchronized Supply Chain Process Management
- VAC Alliance Development
- Product Development

- Shared Service Process Management
- VAC Alliance Development

- Technology Development
- VAC/MetaMarket Alliance Development

- Performance and VAC Process Management
- Bid/Auction Management
- Reintermediation
- MetaMarket Alliance Development
- ASP Infrastructure
- Business Creation Services
- Technology Maintenance/APO

- VAC Alliance Development
- MetaMarket Performance and MetaMarket Process Management
- ASP Infrastructure
- Business Creation Services
- Technology Maintenance/APO

All Companies

- CATE (Continuous Asset Transformation Engine)
- Alliance Development
- Continuous Financial Accounting and Reporting
- e-HR
- e-Management Communication, Performance Review, and Decision Making
- e-Engineering R&D

Figure 3.9 A taxonomy of suggested process models for MetaMarket participants.

common processes. Among these is the CATE, necessary for any MetaMarket participant. Other common processes include rapid alliance development to support continuous disintermediation and reintermediation as well as continuous financial accounting and reporting to support CATE and alliance development. In addition, all the fundamental business processes should be Net-based and e-enabled in order to provide the speed, efficiency, and flexibility required in dynamic MetaMarkets. Any player in a MetaMarket will use the Web for human resources (jobs posting, preliminary interviewing, employee communications, benefits help line), as well as to exchange technical information in the contexts of e-engineering and e-R&D. Players will also use the Web to collaborate on design and prototype development, and to review and agree on design specifications and bring-to-market strategies. E-management, communications, performance review, and decision making will all be Web-based. Relying almost exclusively on Web-enabled processes appears to create an internal culture different from that of traditional companies; there is heightened expectation of speed, flexibility, decisiveness, and rapid information exchange.

Key performance indicators (KPIs) are needed to manage MetaMarket-style companies. Figure 3.10 arrays a series of generic KPIs—the list is only suggestive, not exhaustive—that provide additional perspective on the roles and management objectives of the various MetaMarket players. These KPIs closely track the process taxonomy in Figure 3.9.

Naturally, every player within a MetaMarket shares the objective of driving its own value and market multiples by contributing to year-over-year growth in profits and relative margins, as well as contributing to the discounted cash flow for the MetaMarket. Chapter 6 will more fully examine performance metrics and value parameters for B2B e-businesses and MetaMarkets.

One of the most important concepts and differentiators for the new MetaMarket economy is the degree to which it leverages intellectual capital. Decapitalizing the brand-owning company and leveraging electronic channels to the customer creates a vast range of new options for expanding the business quickly—this is already

Brand-Owning Companies	VAC Supply Chain Participants	VAC Shared Services Participants	Technology Providers	VAC Managers	MetaMarket Managers
• Channel/Option Development	• Supply Chain Metrics (cost, cycle time, reliability)	• Shared Services Metrics	• Installed Base Growth	• VAC Performance (DCF)	• MetaMarket Performance (DCF)
• Customer/Consumer Sales Growth	• Speed of Alliance Development	• Number of VACs	• Number of Participants	• VAC Turnover	• MetaMarket Turnover
• Customer/Consumer Continuity/Stability	• Working Capital Management (inventory, levels/charges)	• Number of VAC Participants	• Stability of Customer Sets	• Number of Network Players	• Number of Network Players
• Speed of Asset Transformation		• Volume/Speed of Transactions		• Transaction Costs	• Volume of Information Flow
• Alliance Stability	• Reserved Capacity Costs				
• Speed of Alliance Development	• VAC Quality				
• Speed of New Product Introduction					

Figure 3.10 Suggested generic key performance indicators.

clear. Worth recognizing is that it also speeds the process of idea actualization by allowing managers in the brand-owning company to focus much more completely on customer requirements and opportunities and on creating MetaMarkets with heightened process optimization and responsiveness. These new-style companies can create new ideas and launch new products and services with vastly more speed than traditional companies, and with far less committed capital. New-style companies can experiment with the market, identify successful new ideas and businesses, and focus capacity on meeting those customer requirements far more quickly and completely than traditional companies. These capabilities are the process basis for the high valuation these companies command: Their array of options for rapidly interfacing with consumers and customers represents value.

Customers have never been so fully integrated into a rapid-response, synchronized supply chain, and they have never had so much control—to specify and receive what they want from the marketplace.

Case Study: Cisco Systems

To illustrate the broad principles and processes of MetaMarkets, the following discussion draws strictly from published information on Cisco Systems. Because companies like Cisco move so quickly, our discussion cannot be viewed as completely up to date, but it does illustrate processes and tactics that Cisco and similar companies have recently used, and it suggests models other companies might explore as they consider founding or participating in a MetaMarket.

Background

Cisco participates in an industry traditionally dominated by large, capital-intensive manufacturing businesses. It is a major player, yet it manufactures virtually none of its products (our examination of

its balance sheet in Chapter 1 explored this level of decapitalization). Cisco is one of four leading competitors—its rivals are
Lucent, Nortel, and Alcatel—that develop, manufacture, market,
and support multiprotocol internetworking systems designed to
link geographically dispersed local and wide area networks. The
company provides access to voice, data, and multimedia applications.

Founded in 1984, Cisco is headquartered in San Jose, California, and has over 26,000 employees. Profits have increased for 41
consecutive quarters and its market capitalization (at $485 billion as
of late February 2000) makes Cisco the second most valuable company in the world, trailing only Microsoft. Cisco has had annual
growth rates between 30 and 40 percent, and expects to continue
growing at this rate. Its customers include businesses of all sizes,
government agencies, utilities, educational institutions, and individual consumers. Telecommunication companies and Internet Service Providers (ISPs) comprise a significant customer segment.
Cisco occupies the number one or number two position in 18 of
the 20 market segments in which it participates.

Cisco has made its mark in communications B2B history by
being first to leverage e-business across the entire value chain. The
company has built an Internet-based network that links its customers, prospects, business partners, and employees. This standards-
based network serves as a platform and foundation for the
deployment of applications. Cisco was among the very first to
demonstrate that B2B e-business is more than selling products over
the Internet. It showed the larger values that can be captured:
Streamlining operations and building relationships with business
partners to reduce costs, speed innovation, provide improved service, and increase customer satisfaction. Essentially, Cisco created a
MetaMarket. At the base of its success was its decision to adopt the
decapitalized, brand-owning model and shed its traditional role as
an equipment manufacturer, choosing instead to concentrate on
core competencies of product innovation, marketing, customer service, and business relationship management.

Global Supply Network Strategy and Processes

In 1992, the company began planning its global supply network strategy. As the chief information officer (CIO) has been quoted, "The Internet is not about putting a thin dot.com veneer on a brick-and-mortar company. It's about fundamentally transforming a company from the inside out" (*Information Week Online*, 2/28/2000). Realizing that growth depended on its ability to scale its manufacturing, distribution, and logistics processes, Cisco management decided to outsource most of that work and use networking technology to link suppliers and distributors closely to in-house processes. These initiatives allow for reduced costs, flexibility in scaling to the market, and a focus on new product development, customer needs, and brand management.

Cisco's supply chain strategy involved five initiatives, including the creation of supply chain and support services VACs:

1. **A single enterprise system.** Creating a single enterprise system that ties together chip manufacturers, electronic manufacturing services, component distributors, logistics partners, Cisco employees, and customers into a single information system. This system enables business partners to manage and operate major portions of the Cisco supply chain. Today, 70 percent of Cisco's production is outsourced and managed by manufacturers, distributors, and logistic partners. The entire supply chain works off the same demand signal; any change in one node of the chain is immediately transferred throughout the chain. This is a formidable demonstration of how disintermediation creates value.

2. **Information sharing in real time.** Allowing market demand signals to flow directly to contract manufacturers without delay, and allowing them to track Cisco's inventory levels in real time. A single information base for demand forecasting reduces inventory and allows for consistent schedules.

3. **Direct fulfillment.** Launching a direct fulfillment model under which most of the company's manufacturing partners can

ship directly to customers. Today, suppliers directly fill 55 percent of Cisco's orders. Customers typically receive the product within three days of manufacturing, and suppliers are directly paid through Cisco's internal systems, thus shortening the gap between expense incurred and expense paid.

4. **Automated testing.** Automating testing to ensure quality by creating test cells on supplier lines and ensuring that the test cells automatically configure test procedures when an order arrives.

5. **Expedited new product introduction.** Expediting new product introduction (NPI) to reduce the number of iterations required during prototype building. As well, automating the process for gathering product data information reduced time-to-market by three months.

Cisco's contract manufacturers, assemblers, distributors, and logistics partners connect with Cisco through Manufacturing Connection Online (MCO), a supply chain portal. This approach essentially positions Cisco as the VAC manager. First deployed in June 1999, MCO provides Cisco and its partners access to real-time manufacturing information including forecast data, inventory, and purchase orders. Creating MCO involved consolidating the access points of numerous manufacturing information systems into a single user interface. Via the company's intranet, Cisco's business partners are able to directly monitor orders from Cisco customers and ship the assembled hardware—without Cisco directly touching an order. The system then prompts Cisco to pay for the parts used.

Once a customer puts an order through, the process is as follows:

1. Order processing links to the scheduling system, which looks at product availability to determine a priority time slot for each order.
2. Component data are then transmitted into orders for Cisco manufacturers and distributors.
3. An electronic commerce application automatically notifies a group of suppliers when incoming orders deviate from forecasts.

4. Improved inventory tracking allows quicker responses to component shortages and the possibility of transferring inventory between different suppliers.

By integrating suppliers earlier in the ordering process, the company has cut delivery time to users from 23 to 10 days. By reducing order-processing costs, inventory costs, errors, and product delivery lead times, and by eliminating low value-added work to improve the productivity of employees involved in purchasing, Cisco has saved $70 million annually in its supply chain process, and its overall costs are down 20 to 28 percent. For 1998 alone, the company estimated that its interconnected supply chain generated $550 million in savings. Growth in the period from 1992 to 1997 of 16× has required minimal headcount increases in manufacturing.

Cisco's supply chain initiatives have eliminated inefficiencies typical of traditional outsourcing, such as paperwork duplication and other labor redundancies that would have burdened both Cisco and its suppliers. The suppliers have also been relieved of the financial burdens of high levels of working capital, inventory, and long order-to-payment cycles, which are typical of less sophisticated supply networks. Prior to the single enterprise strategy, transactions between distributors and manufacturers were not always smooth; there were time lags in delivery and payment and greater opportunity for error. By managing all financial transactions for these exchanges through its enterprise system, Cisco has generated cost savings for its business partners and freed them from low value-added administrative tasks. The quality and speed of product delivery have also improved. By leveraging the Web to link with internal enterprise systems and implementing its supply chain design, Cisco has created value for itself as well as for its suppliers and distributors, all of which clearly positions it as an industry transformer.

Cisco competes for product development and innovation dominance in three ways: in-house R&D investment, outright acquisitions of firms with new technologies, and investment in select companies. It actively partners with small start-ups as well as with large IT firms. What stands out is the rate at which Cisco has been building intellectual capital by acquisition. Since its first acquisition in 1993, Cisco has acquired over 50 companies, averaging between seven and nine acquisitions per year. A review of several recent acquisitions makes the point vividly: Cisco has recently acquired firewall technology (Global Internet Software), virtual private network technology (Altiga Networks), and policy-based networking (Class Data Systems).

We have been speaking so far of the back end. On the front end, Cisco has been equally creative. The company automated customer service through Cisco Connection Online (CCO), a comprehensive resource for customers, suppliers, resellers, and business partners. CCO is essentially a portal to information stored in Cisco's ERP databases, legacy systems, and client server systems, and to more than 1.5 million web pages. CCO has five key components:

- Market-Place—a virtual shopping center
- Technical Assistance and Software Library
- Customer Service for nontechnical assistance
- Internetworking Product Center—a suite of applications for order processing to enable users to configure price, route, and submit orders
- Status Agent—giving Cisco's sales force, direct customers, and partners immediate access to critical information about the status of orders

Cisco has defined customer satisfaction as its primary priority. In its customer self-service model, customers can submit support requests and find answers to frequently asked questions on the Cisco web site. In addition, they can download software updates and diagnostic tolls from the site, get help in an electronic forum, communicate electronically with support staff, and register to receive automatic notification of software bugs and updates.

Cisco's Internet business solutions include a suite of network commerce agents that enable users to configure, price, route, and submit electronic orders directly. These applications are specifically geared to channel partners and key buyers such as value-added resellers (VARs), system integrators, and large buyers. The configuration agent allows more than 10,000 authorized representatives of direct customers and partners to configure Cisco products online. Once the product is configured, customers can obtain pricing information for their selection using the pricing agent. Order Placement allows customers to drop their selections into a shopping cart in Cisco's virtual marketplace. An invoice agent provides customer accounts payable staff with rapid, easy, online access to track their invoices with Cisco. A service order or status agent lets users find information about specific service orders and gives the sales force more timely information, greater control of orders, and increased success with installations. This application also connects users directly to the Federal Express tracking service to determine in real time exactly where their order is in the shipping process. The status agent has transformed the role of sales staff members, who spend less time on clerical tasks such as tracking order status and more time on building client relationships. Cisco's network commerce agents are linked to centralized internal systems that coordinate the entire supply chain and share new product information and engineering changes to inform new product development.

Through CCO and its commerce agents, Cisco has been able to lower the overall cost of taking orders as well as customer frustration caused by inaccurate orders. By automatically trapping errors at the configuration stage, the company has reduced from 15 to 2 percent the number of orders that require reworking. Product delivery lead times have been reduced by two to five days. The use of CCO has resulted in 98-percent accurate, on-time repair shipments and a 25-percent increase in customer satisfaction since 1995.

Cisco Connection Online has allowed Cisco to grow its business and improve the quality of technical support while reducing support costs. The company estimates that close to 70 percent of product ordering is done through the Web, with CCO generating revenues at a run rate of $8 billion per year. Cisco's virtual sales channel presents a real cost advantage against its competitors. More than 80 percent of technical support for customers and resellers is delivered electronically, saving Cisco more than $83 million annually. By distributing 90 percent of its software and documentation electronically, Cisco saves $250 million annually in printing and shipping costs. Overall, CCO saves the company some $350 million per year in operating expense.

Cisco builds alliances with competitors to better service its customers—and theirs. Through this strategy, the company is encouraging industry integration on the customer-facing end. In practice, this proceeds as follows: To accommodate large customers who want to order all of the products for network upgrades from a single source (although they may be supplied by competitors), Cisco has been encouraging companies to install Cisco-powered networks that typically contain about 35 percent Cisco product content. Most consumers are now familiar with the slogan "Intel inside." Cisco is doing the same thing: "Cisco inside" has become a reality. This cooperation is packaged as a win/win situation for customers, who are able to meet all their needs at a single point of sale, and for communications companies that now more easily enter Cisco customers' space.

Cisco's skilled use of supply chain networks and its focus on product development and brand and customer management reflect its external commitment to leadership and its internal effort to ensure a culture where e-business is a top priority for every Cisco employee. The corporate culture is said to emphasize relationship building, speed, flexibility, and innovation. (Other critical measures include meeting customer satisfaction, and sales and performance goals.)

Critical to the success of Cisco's single enterprise strategy is deep information sharing. Cisco needs to ensure its continuous access to all relevant supplier information so that it can intelligently structure relationships among supply chain partners. Typically, these relationships require high levels of daily interaction and problem solving. The same logic applies to product development partners, and of course to customers. Cisco has put in place systems to obtain partner and customer feedback and encourage a corporate culture that looks beyond enterprise walls toward open relationships and information sharing.

IT Strategy

Underlying Cisco's growth has been its information technology strategy. In the early '90s, management made the decision to focus IT on customers rather than on operations and support. First, IT was accordingly moved from the chief financial officer (CFO) organization to a new entity called Customer Advocacy, a business unit responsible for any activity that touches the customer from a service standpoint. One policy corollary to this structural change was that projects would simply not be funded unless they contributed to raising customer satisfaction levels. Second, Cisco required the general managers of operating business units to make the decision concerning which applications to fund. Third, the network would play a strategic role in providing the connectivity necessary for business units to build applications. Cisco built an open, standards-based, enterprise-wide highway, and business units were not required to justify infrastructure investments application by application. Under this structure, IT costs moved out of General and Administrative (G&A) overhead and became a component of cost of goods sold.

Currently, Cisco is assisting its suppliers to Web-enable their internal supply chain processes to further integrate the value chain. The company is also working with its largest customers and resellers to place a Cisco server directly on those customers' premises as part of their own intranet. This server will interface with the customers' enterprise applications and link back to CCO, thus creating a more seamless partnership. Cisco is clearly playing a key role in transforming B2B relationships in the communications industry.

Figure 3.11 provides an overview of how the VACs and Meta-Market managed by Cisco create significant improvements in financial operating results, compared with traditional approaches.

A Comparison of Cisco to Traditional Models

	Traditional	Cisco
Product Cycle Times	5-7 years	6-18 months
Component Sourcing	Many suppliers	Few suppliers more closely coupled
Manufacturing/Assembly	In-house	Outsourced to partners and suppliers, suppliers share risk
Sales Channels	Indirect, many layers	Fewer layers, direct to channel partners and end users
Information Architecture	Unique to firm	"Single Enterprise" architecture continuously shares information among partners
Innovation	In-house	Purchase needed technology or partner to get it if unavailable in-house
Distribution	Company trucks	FedEx trucks, overnight air
Customer Support	High cost center	Self-service, potential revenue center
Customer Contact	9-5 by phone, fax or mail	24x7 on the Web
Size of Firms	Telecom monopolies	Free markets encourage many similar firms, demand economies push consolidation
Intellectual Property	Proprietary networks	Open interoperable standards

Figure 3.11 Cisco's process works through a MetaMarket of three Web-based worlds: Cisco Connection Online (CCO), Manufacturing Connection Online (MCO), and Cisco Employees Connection (CEC), which deals with e-business initiatives that facilitate employee services.

Source: Cisco web site

The Key Learning

The key learning from this case study is clear: Models for VACs and MetaMarkets exist already, and they have proved themselves. The Cisco example is especially instructive because circumstances allowed the company to build virtually a greenfield set of processes and systems. Cisco's competitors arguably have advantages in other areas, such as R&D and manufacturing control. The key strategic question is whether competitors need to transition to a Meta-Market model to achieve additional flexibility, speed, and capital leverage. To our minds, the question is not whether but how major competitors, companies in other industries, and rapidly growing new entrants should go about developing a MetaCapitalist approach. There is an 18-month to 2-year window for companies in most sectors to make this transition in order to emerge as winners in the next decade.

Case Study: A Support Service VAC in Financial Accounting

As noted earlier, companies participating successfully in VACs and MetaMarkets must have transparency, which includes a much more demanding pattern of financial accounting. Continuous financial analysis and reporting and the ability to close books daily in order to participate in rapid alliance development are necessary to support the continuous disintermediation and reintermediation processes of B2B e-business.

The demands are both internal and external. The markets and management are increasingly uninterested in a narrowly historical view of financial performance, reported quarterly and in a full-dress, audited annual report. Instead, they want more continuous, forward-looking performance data, including performance measures that go beyond traditional financial measurement.

Companies are beginning to meet these new demands. Most major companies have created web sites, and they are beginning to release extensive performance data at those sites. Yet even as companies step up to this new demand, the markets are clamoring for still more data, preferably Internet delivered. Further, over the past 10 years most companies have installed more sophisticated IT systems, which provide internally a continuous flow of operating and financial information as well as marketing and customer information. These systems, including ERP and CRM systems, support the data warehouses from which management can obtain more accurate performance measurements. They could also furnish a selection of continuous information and data to external web sites, to satisfy the market appetite for information going well beyond periodic Securities and Exchange Commission (SEC)-mandated disclosures.

As Figure 3.12 indicates, we are speaking here of the transformation of financial accounting. What was once an episodic process of data collection, analysis, auditing, and reporting is fast becoming a continuous process in which data from internal databases and IT systems provide management information and, after due editing, provide the basis for extensive external reporting at a web site. The financial accounting profession will be called on increasingly to manage outsourced financial accounting capabilities for major clients, as well as to carry out its traditional roles—although some participants in MetaMarkets may decide that financial accounting is a core competency and keep much of it in-house. We believe the following to be the principal changes that will transform financial accounting:

- **Traditional audit functions automated.** Traditional audit functions will be automated, drawing information from ERP/CRM and related systems, and will use IT systems with intelligent agents to search for financial and performance anomalies and assess the adequacy of financial controls. The result will be a continuous information flow to management for decision making, as well as an information flow to external Web pages. The externally reported information will be subject to continuous assurance by an independent accounting firm.

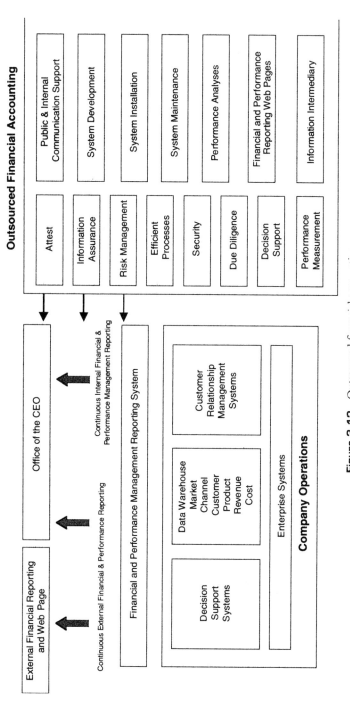

Figure 3.12 Outsourced financial accounting.

- **Closing the books daily.** Financial accounting systems will become dramatically more efficient and books can be closed daily. As noted earlier, companies that need to form alliances and do deals rapidly in the accelerated world of e-business need highly efficient accounting systems and far more financial accounting discipline than in the past.
- **New performance measures.** There will be a new focus on designing metrics for performance measurement under the conditions of MetaCapitalism. Traditional financial information will have its place, as will new operational measures such as the KPIs discussed previously and in Chapter 6. These new performance metrics will need to be closely aligned with the new processes of the B2B companies, be they brand owners or supply chain participants in a VAC.

In sum, decapitalized brand-owning e-business companies will outsource many of their key operational and backroom processes. And one of the largest outsourced components will be financial accounting.

Technology in the Transition to MetaMarkets

It makes sense to conclude this chapter with a brief set of observations about technology in the new B2B world. The section is intentionally brief. An analysis of technology vendors, architectures, solutions, and capabilities would go well beyond the scope of this book, a great deal has already been written, and our focus is business strategy and economics. On the other hand, to offer nothing at all about technology would be misleading: Infrastructure matters enormously in the transition to MetaMarkets.

As Figure 3.13 suggests, the 1990s saw a dramatic rise in enabling technologies within companies. Advances in supply chain, demand chain, and shared services concepts led to process standardization and the implementation of large enterprise systems (ERP and more recently CRM). For the most part, these process changes and systems concentrated on activities within the four

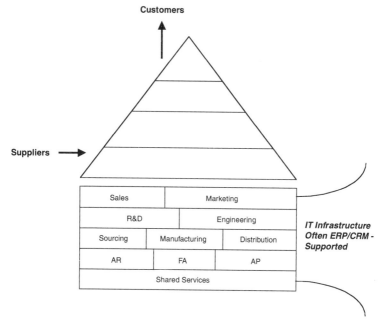

Figure 3.13 Traditional IT overview.

walls of the institution and focused on process efficiency, data availability for analysis and decision making, efficiencies and cost reduction, and the achievement of consistent cost savings in the IT area. Solving the Y2K problem was also on the agenda.

In developing B2B models, technology approaches need to change dramatically to match process changes. Figure 3.14 provides an illustrative framework for technology in a B2B environment. As the figure indicates, technology needs to be applied to create a secure, transparent, high-speed backbone to connect the brand-owning companies with their key strategic partners, their key suppliers, their nonstrategic partners that provide outsourced services, and their technology partners. Figure 3.14 assumes that the brand-owning company is also managing the VAC and MetaMarket network. As discussed in the previous chapter, this may be true in many cases, but not all. Nonetheless, the figure suggests the

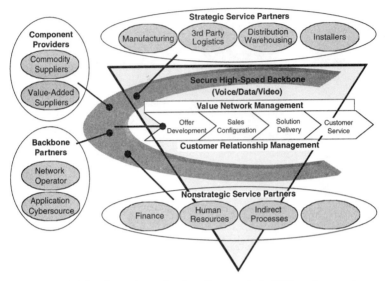

Figure 3.14   Illustrative technology framework for B2B environment.

approach by which technology will knit together the players and conduct transactions.

Figure 3.15 overlays technology applications on this framework. It suggests the key interfaces between existing ERP and SCM systems, the integration of CRM systems, the integration of selected applications and "bolt-ons" for company and network management, the interface with networks through portals, and the eventual connection of customers directly to the supply base. Business-to-business will not initially require a wholesale overhaul of all systems infrastructure. It will build on improvements achieved in the past 20 years.

Globalization

How will MetaMarkets emerge for companies and industries now going through the process of globalization? During the 1980s and 1990s the integration of global capital markets and the focus of

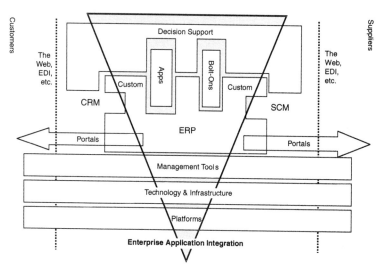

Figure 3.15   High-level technology model for B2B enterprise.

companies on creating global marketing and supply chain strategies accompanied the rise of the Internet. The needed technology evolved to manage complex corporations. Figure 3.16 traces these transitions to their logical point of arrival in global Meta-Markets.

Traditionally, players in the global market structured themselves as multinational companies, with relatively independent entities in each country bound into a corporate structure. These country-based businesses often organized by region and then globally. Because of statutory and local-country public policy frameworks, each country-based business had an independent profit and loss (P&L) statement and a strategy governed by overall corporate strategy. Typically, they had their own approaches to marketing and relatively separate supply chains, sometimes within the framework of an international trade strategy.

Over time, as trade barriers came down and capital markets integrated, companies began to move to a global product model in which the P&L businesses were recast as structures focused around

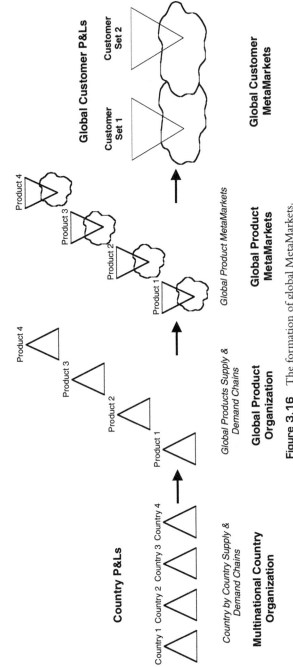

Figure 3.16 The formation of global MetaMarkets.

global products, with global supply and demand chains. This allowed a more coherent global strategy, improved product development and marketing focus, and promoted greater supply chain efficiency.

The MetaMarkets of the coming era will most likely form around these global product structures. MetaMarkets will lead to increased efficiency in supply chain and purchasing transactions and allow companies to focus on global customer sets and global products. However, as global MetaMarkets evolve, they are likely to go through the processes of disintermediation and reintermediation we have already described. As customers learn how to use these networks, and networks respond to "customer-of-one" pressures, MetaMarket businesses will find themselves focused on global customer sets (business or consumer) with appropriate supply and demand chains to drive as much product or service as possible through to the customer sets. MetaMarket businesses will evolve toward maximizing their responsiveness to customer needs.

4

"It's Alive!" The Intelligent Behavior of MetaCapitalist Markets

MetaCapitalism creates dynamic market behaviors. In previous chapters we have described how MetaCapitalism allows companies to leverage financial, human, and brand capital to rapidly pursue broader markets, improve products and services, and enhance the performance of supply chains. This dynamism creates tremendous opportunities for value and wealth creation. However, beyond this dynamism there is a seemingly organic nature to MetaCapitalist markets that makes them even more interesting and exciting: "It's alive!"

In a sense, all markets are organic. When they are well designed, fair, and at least relatively open, they respond to a variety of stimuli and create value. Markets seek to understand the preferences and demands of customers and strive to meet those requirements. Market participants respond to perceived competition for customers, key products and services, and capital with strategies to meet customer requirements and defeat the competition. Over time, markets generally improve their responsiveness in these respects, and market participants that do not improve quickly enough tend to atrophy and are replaced by healthier players.

At the same time that all the players within a market are improving, the structures and rules of the market continue to evolve. An entirely new set of competitive principles may appear, yielding even greater levels of economic growth and wealth. This is arguably an organic, evolutionary pattern: Responding to their environments and the survival issues implicit in those environments, markets mutate over time and generate new hybrids.

And so markets can be viewed as complex adaptive systems. The following significant changes in market structure over the past 20 years confirm this view.

■ Business process reengineering and enhanced supply chain management worked an enormous change in markets. Before these efforts, the key objectives of markets were economies of scale and a push dynamic that emphasized making products and selling them to mass customers. After these efforts, the key objectives became a low cycle time, pull dynamic, and responsiveness to individual customer requirements. New processes ensured that the economics were superior to traditional scale economies. Companies were now able to produce more attractive products and services, at very attractive prices, and to grow without dramatic increases in investment and capacity. In evolutionary terms, a dramatic improvement in the muscular coordination of the traditional industrial infrastructure allowed it to perform tasks with a proficiency unanticipated by earlier economic models. Markets also began to acquire the rudiments of pattern recognition, through data-based marketing, required to move to a still higher level of intelligence.

■ The integration of global capital markets allowed products and funds to flow efficiently on a global basis, creating higher levels of global market efficiency by opening up greater opportunities and permitting capital to find the highest available returns. From an evolutionary perspective, these changes created a far more efficient circulatory system. The overall market organism became quicker in its responses; systems grew and strengthened more rapidly.

- Finally, the ubiquitous application of technology—especially network technology and the Internet—has allowed highly efficient communications and transactional activities to reach across and even create enormous communities. The greater volume of information and greater speed in its communication and in resulting transactions has had massive, positive consequences: Decisions are made quickly, more people participate in increasingly efficient markets, and financial and human capital are leveraged far more effectively. All of which suggests that new markets have acquired a more effective central nervous system. Markets over the past 20 years had already become complex adaptive systems. Today they are dramatically more efficient and responsive adaptive systems.

Figure 4.1 provides a fanciful image of this evolutionary progress. In a sense, systematic changes in markets over the past 20 years have improved the muscular coordination, circulation, and central nervous system that animate a fundamental structure—a skeleton, if you will—that has evolved in the past 200 years of industrial development. Business-to-business e-business and the rise of MetaMarkets create a step-change in the intelligence of markets. And markets can achieve a still higher order of learning, understanding, and adaptation. The pattern of evolution in nature has been characterized as long periods of stability, followed by periods of instability and adaptation. The same thing is happening today. The massive and confused creation of new B2B businesses is a period of instability from which new winners will emerge.

Intelligence? MetaMarkets do appear to be moving from the level of complex adaptive systems to something best described as intelligence. The speed and intensive networking of global MetaMarkets, and their capacity for higher-level functions such as pattern recognition, self-organization, and continuous adaptive mutation, endow MetaCapitalism with characteristics that stretch the imagination. Some of the process and technology features of MetaMarkets suggest the "net-rider" features of a William Gibson cyberspace

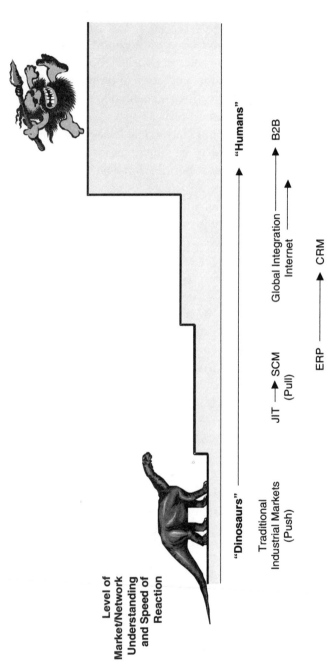

Figure 4.1 Evolution of market intelligence.

novel or the "positronic brain" familiar to fans of *Star Trek*. The technical architecture of MetaMarkets makes clear why this is so. Figure 4.2 provides a high-level schematic of systems architecture and applications that serve to integrate MetaMarkets.

As the figure indicates, MetaMarkets have a series of software applications or functions that increase their capabilities and potential for value and wealth creation. The figure outlines four different types of network functions and capabilities, with an increasing level of value among them. As a network adds these levels of capability, they tend to improve the adaptive behavior and intelligence of the overall network. A summary of these software-based capabilities, from lower order to higher order, would read as follows:

- **Digital content.** Content capabilities can be defined as the underlying data, support, and information databases accessed by network participants to create transactions or exchange informa-

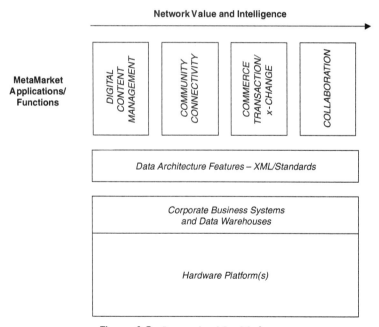

Figure 4.2 Integrating MetaMarkets.

tion. These may include catalogues (part numbers, specification information, SKU descriptions and lists, etc.), financial accounting information, supply chain performance information, help and support information, and information in many other categories. For example, benchmarking databases, market information, and information distributed by trusted third parties, analysts, and rating services might be included. Organizing this information, searching for it, distilling it, and distributing it represent businesses within the network. Some of the content is often thought of as *context*—data patterns and demographics, buying trends, and economics that provide perspective and color to the business data.

- **Community connectivity.** Connectivity software allows members throughout the community (VAC or MetaMarket) to communicate, exchange data, and conduct transactions. Connectivity, often thought of as middleware or enterprise integration applications (EIA), allows enterprises with different software platforms to communicate with each other. Connectivity extracts relevant data and information from various players in the network and allows that information to be accessed by other network players. Connectivity software allows the network to add members and integrate itself, thus creating the overall power and scalability of the network.

- **Commerce transactions.** Commerce applications tend to drive the transactions that occur throughout the network. These may underlie the basic auction approaches in the network or they may be related to value chain activities such as placing orders, billing, and other key transaction elements. The x-change capabilities and features of the network are generally built on the back of commerce applications. The same is true of infomediary services.

- **Collaboration.** Collaborative software allows participants in the network to think and work together nearly in real time. Collaborative software can be used for e-R&D, e-product development, and other business development activities, as well as for Web-based alliance development, business and capacity planning, and other processes where collaboration across a community of interest advances the development of the network, its performance, or its processes. Built on the framework of the other applications and features, collaboration allows the network to behave in an organic style—allows it to be very quick to recognize patterns (market drivers and other forces), review and consider them, develop strategies in response, and execute those strategies. Collaborative software sponsors the formation of global networks. It endows such networks with an unprecedented capacity to leverage human and financial capital, creates the potential for vast new efficiencies, and at best allows networks to react to market forces with a scale and speed never before possible.

Once a network is fully functioning, a relatively small player with a relatively small physical capital base but outstanding intellectual capital can leverage the entire network—yes, in a "bionic" fashion—to understand markets, create products, and deliver to market at levels of scale and efficiency previously impossible even for the largest traditional enterprise. In addition, the applied thinking of an enormous set of network players reviewing market opportunities; collaborating on products or services; understanding the advantages or shortfalls in current product, process, and system solutions; and modifying and changing network responses, creates a collaborative intelligence, reaction speed, and customer responsiveness that far exceed all previous levels.

Especially breathtaking in this transformation of business and industrial models is that B2B networks will allow the transformation to take place quickly—over the next few years. And the organic tendency of the networks to develop will keep them improving. New applications will be added, new approaches will make possible even more intelligence and speed. These in turn will create even higher levels of financial, human, and brand capital leverage. Stepping over the threshold into MetaCapitalism sets in motion market dynamics that accelerate economic growth and wealth creation beyond anything remotely possible within the guarded perimeters of traditional companies.

5

Industry Examples: B2B Transformation and MetaMarket Formation

This chapter offers a series of observations about B2B and Meta-Capitalism as they reshape various industries. We don't propose to provide an in-depth analysis of how MetaCapitalism will transform each industry—that reaches past the scope of our book and the capability of its authors. Industries and markets are changing so quickly that the range of innovative strategies among winning companies is sure to keep us all surprised. However, we can attempt here to illuminate some key features of MetaCapitalism by applying concepts from the two previous chapters to specific corporate and industry settings. This exercise should shine light on possible future evolutionary paths in major sectors. It should also help managers explore alternative approaches to seizing the advantages of the dynamic MetaCapitalist markets of the future.

In earlier discussions we looked at Cisco Systems as a pioneering participant in MetaMarkets and at the beginnings of MetaCapitalist transformation in the automotive industry. We also outlined the ways in which MetaCapitalism could radically alter the lives of companies in service industries such as financial accounting. We could have framed the earlier arguments around such icons as General Motors, Ford, Honeywell International (including former AlliedSignal), General Electric, Chase Manhattan Bank, Dell, Sony, Dupont, or UPS. These companies and many, many others are attacking the market with the means of MetaCapitalism, even if they do not yet have this term in their lexicon.

We are still in the early stages of this revolution. The MetaCapitalism rocket has ignition, and it is just beginning to rise from the launching pad. Figure 5.1 provides a view from Goldman Sachs on the distribution of B2B by industry segment. The analysis suggests that the chemicals industry, for example, may have a high density of B2B transactions because of its many independent players, its relatively effective trading and transmission networks, and the interchangeability of many of its raw materials and by-products. On the other hand, computer and networking companies may also turn out to be major players in the B2B revolution: They provide many of the important building blocks, and—witness Cisco— many have converted their internal processes to network-based approaches. Newly configured, they can be e-businesses as well as major players in the transformation.

Figure 5.2 addresses the problem somewhat differently but arrives at similar results. This analysis by Forrester Research suggests that motor vehicles may play a larger role in future B2B enterprises, probably because of the millions of parts and the range of materials that feed into the industry. Also notable in the Forrester analysis is the B2B strength of the utilities industry.

Nonetheless, both of these charts offer only a preliminary analysis. In our view, the charts miss the leverage of financial and human capital through B2B and also the dynamic optimization of

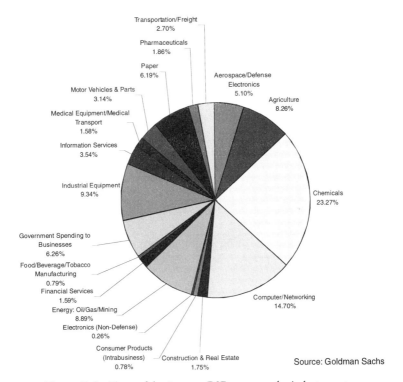

Figure 5.1 Share of the Internet B2B economy by industry sector.

MetaMarkets, all of which will drive economic growth at unprecedented rates. From our perspective (outlined in the next chapter), B2B will be fully transformational. It will have an economic impact on the order of $200 trillion rather than the $10 to $20 trillion estimates captured in most recent analyses.

In the industry-specific discussions in this chapter it will be apparent that, as first steps toward organizing VACs, many industry leaders and market makers are creating market site portals similar to that in Figure 5.3. Because the originators of these portals differ widely from one another (industry leaders, supplier groups, new entrants), the business models implicit in the design of these portals will focus on a wide variety of new market opportunities. Most of these opportunities will be disintermediated as the networks

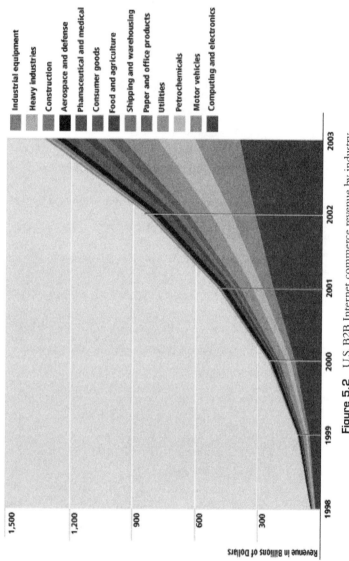

Figure 5.2 U.S. B2B Internet commerce revenue by industry.

Source: Forrester Research

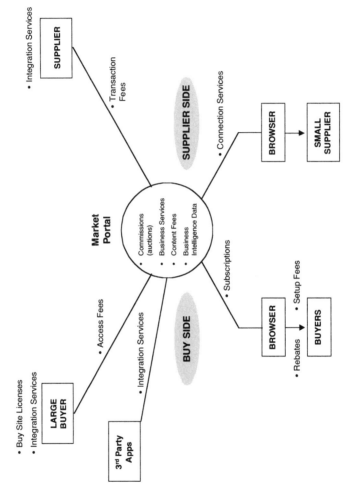

Figure 5.3 Business structure map for B2B portals.

mature into fully functioning VACs and MetaMarkets with more integrated structures.

Manufacturing: the Automotive Industry

In Chapter 1 we explored the transition of automotive industry leaders from original equipment *manufacturers* to vehicle *brand owners*. General Motors and Ford are moving rapidly to create Internet-based approaches as first steps toward an automotive MetaMarket. At this stage, they appear to be using the Internet to install more advanced EDI, an automated bidding system, and processes to improve the efficiency of their supply chains.

General Motors has created a new unit, e-GM, to inject e-commerce throughout its business. Initially, this supplier-focused initiative is dedicated to expanding the global purchasing system that General Motors has used in recent years to negotiate discounts from its vendors and drive greater efficiency throughout its external supply chains. The GM Market Site is not intended to attract other automotive manufacturers, and the operation is not expected to be spun off. However, it is entirely possible that GM may use the site to create and manage its own MetaMarket. GM's partner, Isuzu Motors, will soon convert its entire purchasing system to operate through the GM Market Site, which contains a catalog function with 200,000 items available to GM and its suppliers through five participating companies. The site is powered by Commerce One's Market Site global portal solution, which automates supplier transactions from order through payment. It also utilizes Commerce One's BuySite electronic procurement applications.

GM Market Site will operate in conjunction with GM Supply Power, a new Internet portal that promises to improve the company's supply chain integration. GM estimates that processing orders via the Internet will reduce the cost of processing and managing purchase orders from $100 to $10. The company also estimates that within a few years this site alone could be handling annual sales of as much as $500 billion. These sites and their auction functions are a part of GM's Global Asset Recovery Program. GM has conducted the automotive industry's first Internet-based B2B auction on GM Trade Exchange. Its first purchasing orders totaled more than $500 million in MRO sourcing.

GM is in a fierce race with Ford to streamline its supply chain processes as a first step toward creating a MetaMarket and becoming the market maker in auto parts and supplies. Ford's Auto-Xchange is designed to streamline supply chain processes for Ford and its tier one suppliers. Through heightened supply chain efficiency and synchronization, it will operate as a make-to-order pull system rather than a make-to-stock push system. In a joint venture with Oracle, Ford is ramping up to manage Ford's direct supply chain of $80 billion a year and its extended supply chain of $300 billion a year. Ford manages AutoXchange as a business—with billions of transactions and an auction function for itself and its suppliers. The company will also earn fees for managing the extended supply chain for other firms that use it.

All of these initiatives at Ford represent important steps in the direction of creating and managing VACs as well as creating and managing an overall MetaMarket. In the minds of Ford strategists, the longer-range evolution of these concepts is to extend the supply chain capabilities to functions such as warranty, performance, and design collaboration, and to make these systems the backbone that will eventually connect Ford customers directly with its suppliers.

These strategies may continue to evolve. GM, Ford, and DaimlerChrysler AG, along with GM partners Suzuki Motor Company and Isuzu Motors, Ltd., Ford's Mazda unit, and competitors Commerce One and Oracle, are all investing in a new, integrated automotive parts exchange. Toyota Motor Corporation is considering joining, as well. Cost efficiencies from running reverse auctions to elicit the lowest bid on a part are the most obvious but perhaps smallest drivers of anticipated value. The supply chain efficiencies that automation confers—obviating the need for myriad phone calls, meetings, and mountains of blueprints and paper spec faxes—promise to add enormous value and cut down product development time.

Most critically, management attention at each competing/collaborating car company can now focus on the principal driver of the new B2B paradigm: becoming a more competitive vehicle brand owner (VBO) and competing more effectively for larger bases of ever-more-loyal customers. Paradoxically, by collaborating on automating the back-end B2B processes, more focus can be applied to structuring independent solutions in a more keenly competitive arena. We are now a step closer to the prediction about this industry we first made in *Wisdom of the CEO:* A more efficient market will accelerate the consolidation of the sector to five or so nameplate car companies.

For the collaborators, the gloves are off. For nonparticipants in the emerging parts MetaMarket, consequences are dire: Entry barriers to a perfected parts market are higher than ever, putting their very survival as independent organizations at risk.

These moves all represent short-term tactics and raise fresh strategic questions for the industry. Will the new, large parts Xchange survive antitrust and price-fixing challenges? Will it master and manage its sheer complexity? Will the major automakers decide to return to independently managed MetaMarkets as they begin to spin off a greater share of production, and customer ownership is increasingly disintermediated? These issues frame some of the most important strategic questions for MetaCapitalism in the automotive sector.

Figure 5.4 summarizes the current state of this far-reaching transformation of the automotive industry. Within the next few years, annual transaction levels should exceed several trillion dollars. A vast sum—yet these networks represent only the initial stages of transformation. Their principal purpose is to use the Internet to improve EDI linkages to suppliers, streamline supplier auctions with the OEM, among themselves and with external markets, and drive down overall transaction costs. In our view, this is a somewhat limited menu. The networks do not yet take sufficient advantage of the dynamic potential of MetaMarkets to completely transform the industry.

Figure 5.5 begins to suggest the promise and additional payoff

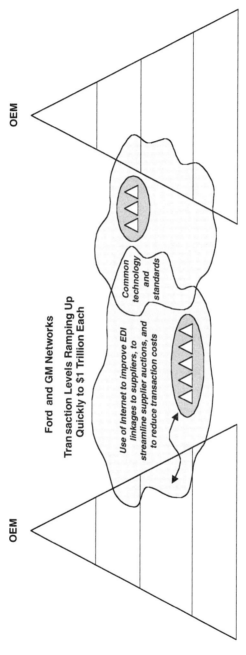

Figure 5.4 Establishing B2B networks in the automotive industry.

of building automotive MetaMarkets. Once the initial networks are completed and supply chains reach a higher level of efficiency, the stage will be set for more rapid disintermediation of the OEMs and outsourcing of some major processes. GM has defined its networks as part of an overall Global Asset Recovery Program. Properly managed, such a program might evolve into a disintermediation process, in preparation for the company becoming a VBO. Successfully carried out, this transition would generate greater leverage of financial and human capital, focused more completely on the customer, following a process model much like the decapitalized brand-owning models explored in the previous chapter.

In addition, automotive MetaMarkets are likely to evolve toward taking greater advantage of the optimization dynamics of VACs and MetaMarkets. As initially conceived, these exchanges knit together the supply chains of traditional supply bases, combined with some additional captive suppliers who may begin to compete with the traditional sources. Over time, MetaMarket dynamics might open up the supply base to a broad range of new entrants, allowing virtually all qualified companies to participate in the auction process. Were these new participants significantly superior to current suppliers, they would have the opportunity to replace them. Although this dynamic process would create more complex supplier relationships and make parts and systems catalogs more subject to change, a well-designed MetaMarket should be able to manage this level of complexity and provide far higher levels of efficiency and responsiveness to the vehicle brand-owning companies.

Finally, the exchanges need to be stretched into full Meta-Markets so that they can enhance customer contact and begin to connect the customer to the entire supply and demand chain. Customers are already experiencing a hint of this through online automotive purchasing systems. The vehicle brand-owning companies will be in a position to leverage these electronic networks and channels even more effectively to deliver additional products and services to consumers.

What will be the result? The conversion of a highly capital-

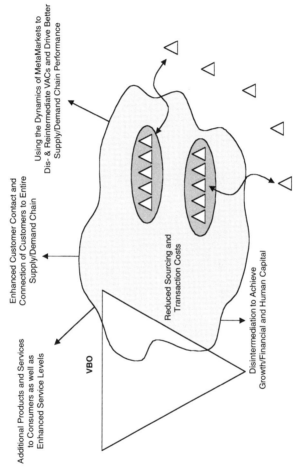

Additional Products and Services to Consumers as well as Enhanced Service Levels

Enhanced Customer Contact and Connection of Customers to Entire Supply/Demand Chain

Using the Dynamics of MetaMarkets to Dis- & Reintermediate VACs and Drive Better Supply/Demand Chain Performance

VBO

Reduced Sourcing and Transaction Costs

Disintermediation to Achieve Growth/Financial and Human Capital

Figure 5.5 The future promise and payoff of automotive MetaMarkets.

intensive industry into a fast-moving, flexible industry with an evolutionary path that simply cannot be predicted, even over the next five years. Nothing illustrates the excitement and challenges of the B2B revolution more than the promise it offers to the automotive industry.

Manufacturing: Chemicals

Another important example in the manufacturing sector is the chemical industry. Several analyses suggest that chemicals will be one of the leading industries in B2B transactions, at least during the early phases of the B2B revolution. The principal reasons for this are the complexity of the current market structure and the inevitable complexity of any future MetaMarket structure. The complexities in today's market include a vast array of small players feeding the larger companies, the interchangeability of many feeder chemicals, the assortment of by-products that become ingredients for other chemical processes, and the complex interfaces between the chemical industry, pharmaceuticals, oil and gas, and utilities. Small changes in costs or demand can lead to significant shifts in the economics of the value chains and in purchasing decisions across each of these interfaces. Because the purchasing decisions are complicated and prices fluctuate significantly, an enormous amount of information and economic modeling is needed to make appropriate business decisions.

For all these reasons, the chemical industry and its trading partners are ripe candidates for MetaCapitalist transformation—for the formation of interconnected MetaMarkets, greater supply chain efficiency, reduced transactions costs, and closer integration of ultimate customers with the supply chain. As Figure 5.6 demonstrates, it would have been very hard to tackle this network of industries without the communications capabilities, analytic power, and transparent transaction capabilities offered by the Internet.

As with the auto industry, initial efforts to organize this industry around the B2B model are focused on purchasing and market

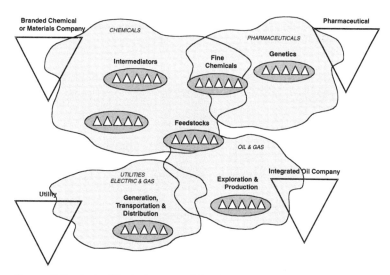

Figure 5.6   A simplified schematic of the chemicals and related MetaMarkets.

making. Figure 5.7 illustrates the web sites of a variety of market makers, each focused on a different aspect of the chemical industry, with differing product catalogs and different ultimate users. The formation of these market makers begins to create an EDI backbone for the industry. With this backbone, it will be easier to go on to form more dynamic VACs, which can emphasize cost, quality, and reliability and begin to dominate auctions within the industry. Over time, a MetaMarket will begin to connect end users directly into this complex supply chain and, in many cases, force branded chemicals producers to disintermediate, decapitalize, and focus on product development and customer management. Some of these major players will probably also take over management of the MetaMarket.

All of this represents an enormous transformation of a traditional, complex industry. It also carries with it the promise of faster product innovation, development, and delivery; higher-quality products in what many consider a commodity industry; and a simplification of the industry to reduce transaction costs and, ultimately, consumer prices.

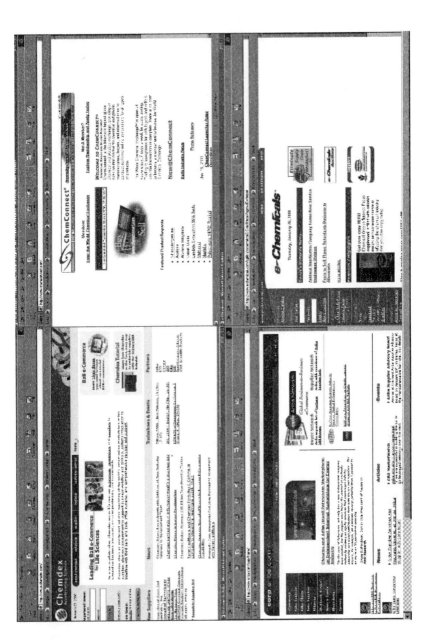

Figure 5.7 Sample chemical market makers.

Perhaps a simple illustration will shed further light. Several years ago we made a study of supply chain management and just-in-time techniques applied to the nylon fiber and carpet business. Thanks to JIT and other performance improvement methods, the normal six-week cycle time (produce nylon fiber, dye the fiber, produce the carpet, warehouse it, distribute to retailers) was in the process of being shortened to six days (order carpet, produce and spin dyed nylon, produce carpet, ship directly to consumer). The Internet can transform this process even more dramatically (consumer designs carpet on the Internet, manufacturer dyes and spins nylon, produces carpet, delivers to consumer within several days). A small example— but it hints at the power of e-business to change the economics, processes, and customer responsiveness of major industrial sectors and focus worldwide electronic markets on customers of one.

B2C Retailing

The transformation of the retail industry is moving forward at a furious pace. The formation of a vast array of new, Internet-based retail options (i.e., B2C: business-to-consumer), aligned with or competing with traditional catalog and brick-and-mortar establishments, has been widely reported. During the Christmas holidays of 1999, Internet-based retail shopping increased three- to fivefold over the previous year—from $3.3 billion in 1998 to a number we estimate at $10 billion, while the high estimates of other surveys reach as far as $14 billion. During this period, U.S. Postal Service priority mail volume increased by 20 percent and specialty logistics and fulfillment systems reported year-over-year increases of 65 to 70 percent. Leading specialty retailers indicated that e-retail sales volume for the 1999 to 2000 Christmas season was up between 400 to 500 percent over the previous year.

Consumers are becoming comfortable with online shopping; timely fulfillment and package delivery are now the limiting factors. However, solutions are being developed for scaling up and smoothing out logistics and distribution systems, and the physical

movement of products should be able to keep up with the exponential rise in online ordering. In our view, retailers will soon be
faced with becoming MetaMarket or VAC managers for consumer
goods—or falling by the wayside as immensely more effective mer-
chandizing models appear.

The Entertainment, Media, and Telecom Industries

It is no secret that new technology, new products, and changing
consumer tastes, as well as basic economics, are leading to a dramatic convergence and integration of the entertainment, media,
and telecommunications industries. Nor is it a secret that during
the next few years hundreds of billions of dollars will be invested by
telecoms and others in building Internet Protocol (IP) networks
and installing related broadband technology. Many features of this
convergence lie outside the scope of this book, but here too VACs
and MetaMarkets—the building blocks of MetaCapitalism—will
dominate. And this we need to investigate.

At an early stage of this transformation, many telecoms adopted
the dual strategy of achieving a large customer base in long distance
and local carriage while moving aggressively toward broadband
capability. As carriers have built the infrastructure and the process
model to carry broadband Internet information from any point in
the world to any other point at the lowest possible cost, they have
merged in order to extend their networks. As well, they have
moved to broadband strategies (cable, fiber optic, and wireless), and
they have entered into alliances with content producers (motion
picture and television studios, publishers, etc.) and technology firms
(network software and hardware, set top boxes, etc.). Although
many of these businesses compete against each other for the same
customers, and this has caused some degree of organizational confusion and brand dilution, in the initial phases most of the companies have nevertheless managed these technologies as independent
businesses with independent P&Ls.

Similarly, entertainment and media companies have broadened their offerings in both content development and delivery and have often become complex businesses that include motion picture production and distribution, television production, television networks, music production and distribution, publishing and distribution, cable TV, theme parks, retail stores, and packaged consumer products distribution. As in the case of the telecoms, each of these businesses is typically managed in the traditional way as an independent business competing with all the others, but this approach often fails to fully leverage brand potential and leads to some degree of consumer and brand confusion.

Then along comes the Internet. As the Internet user population grows and there are surges both in personal computer (PC) sales and in the uses of the Internet and intranets for a vast new variety of consumer and business needs, Internet service companies are being created with dramatically different business models. As Figure 5.8 suggests, the traditional companies with their large P&L businesses, large capital bases, and relatively large amounts of working capital, still adhere to the traditional corporate model. Examples might well have been any of the telecoms and the entertainment giants such as Time Warner.

On the other side of the table are the Internet companies such as AOL, concentrating less on their physical capital base, more on attracting customers to their electronic networks and services, and retaining customers once acquired. As the market assesses the potential of these widely different types of companies, it assigns a traditional multiple to entertainment and media companies and telecoms and a very high multiple to Internet companies, based on the view that the latter will achieve the promise of MetaCapitalism. When mergers join the two types of companies, it should be no surprise that the value of Internet companies declines as they blend with traditional businesses, while the value of traditional businesses increases. The market is willing to reward the promise of a more rapid transformation of traditional businesses into MetaCapitalist businesses.

The newly merged institutions will have to work hard to seize

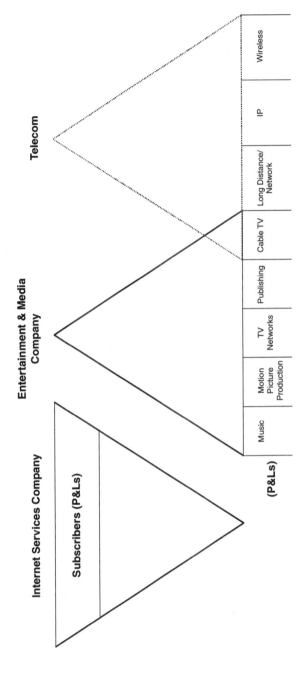

Figure 5.8 Entertainment, media, and telecom integration.

their opportunity. As Figure 5.9 indicates, such companies are initially a hodgepodge of customer-focused P&L businesses and businesses focused on products, services, and channels. While each of these business units can continue to be managed independently and compete against its traditional rivals, the market has rewarded the overall company in anticipation of aggressive transformation, and it will treat the company harshly if its operating units don't restructure to address the New Economy aggressively.

The right side of Figure 5.9 provides an illustration of how dramatic this transformation needs to be. To grow the value of the new company, these enormous merged entities must quickly adopt a MetaMarket model (either virtual—without outsourcing, or real—with outsourcing) in which its businesses are converted into VACs, some devoted to content production, others to delivery channels.

During this reorganization, customer-facing businesses that control P&Ls and asset allocation are formed around customer sets. These may be *consumer* customer sets focused on specific consumers, with demographics or other characteristics that suggest a

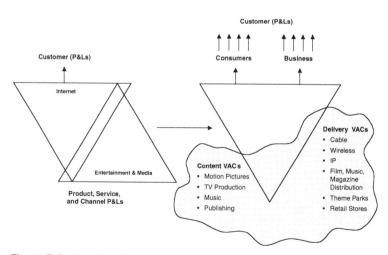

Figure 5.9 Securing the value: creating the entertainment, media, and telecom MetaMarket.

coherent market target. They may also be *business* customer sets, structured either along industry lines or by business size or other characteristics. These customer-focused business units can determine customer demands and requirements and create packages of services drawn both from content VACs and from channel VACs to assure coherent, integrated, branded services targeted on customer needs. When this occurs, customers will come to regard the company as their foremost delivery agent for a vast array of services. Further, the business units will continuously focus on using the content and channel engines to drive ever higher levels of service and business to each customer set.

The content and channel engines will generally need to be managed as cost centers. While they may have shadow P&Ls, it is important that they not behave as independent business entities as long as they remain within the four walls of the company. Were they to behave as independent entities, internal politics would lead to a misalignment of corporate resources and excessive competition, and this in turn would eventually waste capital, confuse the customer, and reduce brand loyalty. The customer-focused P&L business unit leadership need to oversee resource allocations and investment strategy for each of the content and channel VACs to assure their alignment with market and customer requirements.

Over time, of course, this approach could lead to a disintermediation of the company into a content and channel MetaMarket managed by the brand-owning company. Within the MetaMarket, content and channel VACs would behave as businesses, and would participate in auctions as the customer-focused P&L business leaders assemble the appropriate content and channels for their products. This business model would in turn drive the cost, reliability, and optimized responsiveness that underlies efficient MetaMarket performance.

The problem is that the market is not fully convinced that these large new companies, recently merged, can pull off this organizational and management transformation and thereby secure the value promised by MetaCapitalism. The restructuring of P&Ls in these enormous businesses, the reorganization, the redeployment of management requires tremendous vision and leadership. In some instances, management teams may lack the vision or sheer management skills to succeed. As in many management transformations, the faster these changes are accomplished, the better. Such massive change entails risks to the business, of this there can be no doubt. Offsetting this risk, however, is the greater risk that the newly merged companies may have all the elements to be premier players in new MetaMarkets—yet fail to formulate the appropriate strategy and fail to execute, thus creating overwhelming opportunity costs. This level of challenge takes us back to elements of the relativity equation with which this book began: change × courage. Management insight into change and the courage to manage change at high speed are essential.

Financial Services

MetaCapitalism creates new patterns of capital generation and flow, as well as new sources and measures of value. And for these reasons it demands entirely new financial products and creates new institutions. In recent years, the focus in financial services has been on products (mix and profitability) and distribution/channels, with an associated focus on risk management and scale economies. The financial services sector is in the midst of a dramatic consolidation to create a broader economic base to address these issues as well as generate the capital and reach to succeed in an ever growing and changing market.

At the level of the financial institution, the Internet opens up the opportunity to extend these strategies. The movement toward virtual financial services via the Internet and related technologies should accelerate the transformation away from highly capitalized physical interfaces with the individual and corporate customer (brick and mortar institutions) toward electronic and computer-based interfaces. As in the manufacturing sector, this should allow for more rapid product design and introduction, innovation, variety, convenience, and better use of time. It should also lower costs, owing to pricing and terms arbitrage, higher efficiency of capital markets in this model, and scale economies.

The Internet model accelerates the movement of capital to sources of highest return by providing better information on investment opportunities and a much enhanced capacity to move capital quickly. While it creates a much tougher and more competitive market, it also provides larger and more varied sources of funding for attractive investment opportunities.

By way of example, Figure 5.10 illustrates how electronic brokerage and trading may be affected over the next several years: at the front end of Internet brokerage with a dramatic rise in both accounts and managed assets, at the back end with a dramatic rise in electronic trade settlement. As suggested in the next chapter, some of these initial forecasts may turn out to be very conservative.

Similarly, the Internet accelerates economies of scale by providing a much larger market for savings, investment, loan, credit, and insurance products. In addition, as the capital markets are further integrated by the Internet and become more transparent and

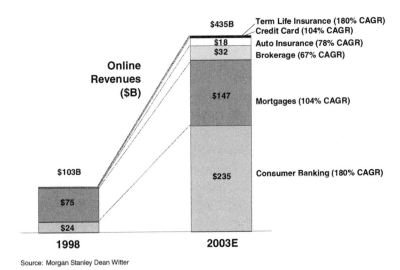

Source: Morgan Stanley Dean Witter

Figure 5.10 B2C e-business will experience exponential growth.

efficient, scale economies are created in areas such as foreign exchange, custody, and other areas of transaction mechanics. The impact of these changes is suggested in Figure 5.11. A tremendous surge in online revenues should occur over the next few years, reflecting enormous growth in everything from life and auto insurance to mortgages and consumer banking. Disintermediation should allow substantial transaction efficiencies as well as dramatic improvement in the customer's ability to shop and select preferred financial offerings.

Finally, in areas such as investment and merchant banking, the Internet facilitates review of deals and opportunities and creates a vastly larger, potentially global pool of opportunities from which to select the most attractive. Again, this should dramatically add to the efficiency of the capital markets. It will also all but force a major improvement in management capability and performance. The new efficiency, integration, and growth of capital markets (see the figure on page 134), combined with the discipline of continuous financial reporting described earlier, will generate a new financial infrastructure and make greater demands on individual experience and skill.

Electronic Retail Brokerage & Trading Execution Penetration

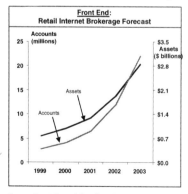
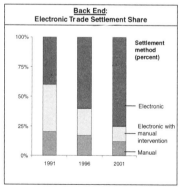

Source: Forrester Research, Tower Group, PwC analysis

Figure 5.11   Automated operations are already penetrating the entire value chain.

In short, the application of Internet technology to the financial services sector, combined with the dramatic opening up and integration of global capital markets in the 1990s, will transform the sector and lay the foundation for dramatic accelerated growth in the world economy.

Figure 5.12 provides a high-level, admittedly rough interpretation of how MetaCapitalism will affect the financial services industry. The figure highlights the movement away from bricks and mortar as the principal market channel to customers. It also points to the creation of a MetaMarket encompassing VACs for wholesale services, retail products and services, and transactions. The dynamics of the MetaMarket again foster waves of new services, lowered costs, and improved transaction efficiencies (e.g., foreign exchange, custody, trading). In addition, the figure illustrates the disintermediation process in which consumers and businesses can increasingly deal directly with the providers of products and services. They become participants in a wholesale market, and a vast array of brokerage and service functions is simply cut out.

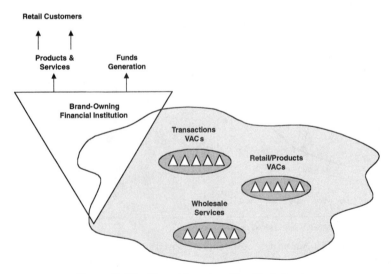

Figure 5.12   Financial services MetaCapitalization.

The implications of these changes in financial services are enormous:

- MetaCapitalism brings the technology, facilities, and market access previously enjoyed by professional traders in whole-sale markets to individuals managing their own money at home. It will increasingly disintermediate professionals.
- Organizations, banks, and insurance companies that do not embrace this model will have difficulty improving the broad economics of their businesses. If they do not transition customers quickly enough, incumbents will fail. Channel costs are a fraction of the cost of traditional methods. For this and many other reasons, customer power will drive prices through the floor and current practices such as credit card interest levels will disappear or be considered extortion.
- On the Net, a price play will not be good enough. The battle will be fought on service, product innovation, interest generated, and knowledge. The linking of the Web front end to existing processing systems will be the customer service Achilles' heel of major traditional players. Advice and knowledge, as well as VAC and MetaMarket management, will be the competitive frontier.
- Global MetaMarkets will accelerate cross-border marketing to financial services customers and servicing of those accounts. This will vastly accelerate the integration of the European market, despite regulatory and other attempts to slow or prevent that process in some respects. Scale will help and hinder: It will help with cost, hinder in agility and service.
- Regulatory crises cannot be entirely avoided. We will enter a period of more extensive regulation, requiring greater transparency and disclosure of cross interests.
- Large swathes of the wholesale financial system will be transformed by the accelerating globalization of capital markets and the popularization of equities and risk sharing. The dynamics of MetaMarkets will cause reengineering to take

place at lightning speed to respond to rapidly restructuring markets and the changing demands of customers. No country will be able to afford to ignore the liquidity provided.

Speed, efficiency, and transparency will transform the financial services industry worldwide. In turn, this great industry will become one of the key enablers of accelerated business growth and wealth creation worldwide.

Higher Education

We are all aware that colleges and universities are now "wired," but the transformation of higher education is far from complete. The further evolution of higher education will offer, we are certain, an important illustration of e-business methods at work. E-business approaches have tremendous potential in a service sector that traditionally delivers information through capital-intensive channels (human and physical capital)—so much so that we predict major transformation in the sector, which has remained essentially unchanged since the founding of universities in the Middle Ages. We believe that all education—elementary, secondary, higher education, continuing education—will quickly become Net based. Only in this way will it be possible to enhance consistency, quality, and currency, and prepare students to participate creatively in a world that is quickly transforming on the basis of the Internet and MetaCapitalism.

While acknowledging that many societies are entering into a "K through 99" educational environment, we will focus here on higher education. In this sector a set of highly successful institutions delivers a product through a model that is roughly comparable in structure, worldwide. However, the word *product* already lofts a warning flare. Many faculty members and administrators may prefer to confine to the business and admissions offices of their institutions such concepts as markets, customers, demand, supply, capacity, costs, and pricing, not to mention profit. To ignore these realities is neither possible nor fruitful—not now, and not in the coming era of Internet-mediated MetaMarkets. Education cannot help but change. In addition, business concepts will be increasingly relevant as for-profit enterprises soon begin to deliver the higher education product via the Internet and related technologies, and challenge the position of traditional not-for-profit institutions of higher education.

On the whole, the revolution in the retail sector is visible. Front-page coverage about the battles between Amazon.com and Barnes & Noble, between eToys and Toys 'R' Us, has made everyone keenly aware of the dramatic changes unleashed by the Internet. In contrast, changes in educational process—and potential changes—are less obvious. Professors continue to lecture and facilitate discussions. Students continue to be challenged to develop their capacity for critical thinking. Education continues to be delivered face-to-face in small seminars, standard classrooms, and lecture halls. A world in which the Internet delivers serious components of education is nearly unthinkable to most faculty members. Heated debates, even protests, about the impact of technology are occurring in every corner of the university, and for obvious reasons: In the brave new world impending, technology can disintermediate faculty.

In an unchanging world, the faculty members would be right. The richness of face-to-face educational experience in comparison with technology-mediated learning needs no defense: It is an obvious good. However, the world is not unchanging. Those institutions that stand still will do so at their peril.

We believe that higher education will be required to follow the MetaCapitalist model, and base this assumption on an assessment of the pressures and stresses currently facing higher education. Most projections suggest that even at current pricing assumptions (current tuition levels), higher education will have an excess demand of several hundred thousand students per year over the next several decades. This excess is caused by the inability to build classrooms and physical plants quickly enough to keep pace with demand in the developed and developing countries. However, if the use of technology could dramatically lower the cost of education while providing greater educational capacity, the level of excess demand could surge still more, into the millions per year worldwide, yet high-quality education could be provided to all who aspire to it.

Today, over 65 percent of all jobs are skilled, in contrast to only 20 percent of all jobs in 1950. Yet only one person in 100 in the world has a college education. Even those with college degrees find that the shelf life of their degrees is shrinking. To advance in their careers, lifelong learning is a necessity, and the numbers bear this out: Today nearly 50 percent of all students are over the age of 25, compared with only 25 percent in 1970. It will be virtually impossible to build enough brick-and-mortar institutions to meet this explosion in demand. Like it or not, technology-mediated learning will be the strategic response to meet this demand. The investment community is already savvy to this huge profit opportunity, and the influx of capital into the sector is just the spark needed to ignite the fire.

- On college campuses, a concept known as the 1-percent (cost) solution is beginning to replace faculty-mediated courses with technology-mediated ones at a fraction of the cost. The new math of e-business applied to higher education is straightforward. Recent studies suggest that 25 to 30 course titles represent in excess of 80 percent of most undergraduate education. Numerous new business ventures have already been launched to attract the best faculty and "content providers" in each of these subject matter areas to create two-way Internet-based education on a worldwide basis. The concept is to surround the very best faculty and content providers with leading education and entertainment content packagers and producers. The result is intended to be high-quality, entertaining, student-paced interactive content, available worldwide.

- It is only a matter of time before the experience of technology-mediated instruction is enhanced through still further waves of new technology. Increasingly, online education will move up the "richness chain." More and more elements of the curriculum will be delivered by technology. The economies of scale and attractiveness of this model are obvious. The ability of an institution to provide the highest-quality educational content in the most interesting and informative packaging for a fraction of current tuition cost will not go unnoticed. Those who successfully complete their course work in this form and demonstrate their competence will receive credit and, in due course, their degrees from highly reputed institutions offering the courses.

There are additional markets in our new K–99 world of learners. The rising importance of distance learning, executive education, and the need of people of all ages to acquire knowledge and skills available through institutions of higher education suggest even greater demand for training, courses, and degrees. Clearly, there will be a first-mover advantage for those who address these needs.

Figure 5.13 provides a partial illustration of the dynamics behind the application of MetaCapitalism to higher education (or for that matter, to any level of education). The traditional college and university system is massively decentralized: Tens of thousands of professors and instructors, in thousands of colleges and universities, produce individualized content and packaging for classes of 5 to 200 students. Content, quality, and presentation vary tremendously, and the results from the students' perspective vary just as much. While some consistency is achieved through standard textbooks, admission, degree, and certification requirements, academic exchanges, and other means, the approach is nonetheless quite fragmented—and means to be so. However, the economics underlying this structure are difficult, with very large physical plants supporting these activities and demand of all sorts greatly exceeding supply.

The right side of Figure 5.13 suggests the creation of a Meta-Market for educational content. It would be composed of a set of content VACs, perhaps 25 to 30 in number, corresponding to the most sought-after university courses. Each VAC would focus on creating the best content in its topic area, packaging that content in the most congenial and useful fashion, and developing consistent course sequences (curriculum) and testing. The competitive dynamics of any MetaMarket would apply here: Both the VACs and the MetaMarket would be open to new entrants offering better content or better delivery.

The creation of such a MetaMarket would generate a new role for universities. The electronically mediated audience for higher

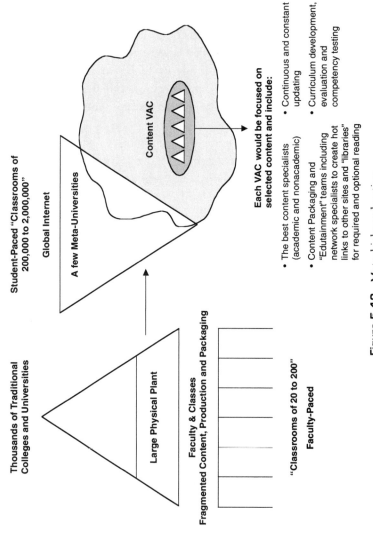

Figure 5.13 Meta-higher education.

education would be vastly larger than the current audience. The new economics of higher education MetaMarkets would almost certainly prompt a major consolidation among institutions of higher education. It would also provoke a systematic decapitalizing of university structures and large physical plants, which would become less necessary. Some universities would become the organizers and managers of educational MetaMarkets. They would appraise the content and delivery quality of various content-focused VACs; organize the process for consistent delivery to students; and oversee broad-based competency testing, competency requirements for degrees, and the awarding of degrees.

The economics of higher education would be dramatically transformed. Today's university serving an undergraduate population of 10,000 students, with an annual operating budget of $350 to $500 million and tuition ranging from $20,000 to $30,000 per year, might find itself serving a student population of 200,000 to 300,000. It would manage a MetaMarket of 50 content and delivery VACs, each funded at between $10 and $20 million per year (economic models more closely resembling television production than higher education today), with a total operating budget between $500 million and $1 billion and annual tuition per student in a range between $1,500 and $3,000.

In terms of curriculum quality, many students might find the high-quality packaged presentations and carefully paced delivery to be enormously attractive, offering a rapid route toward subject matter competency. These values, combined with low tuition, should more than compensate for the absence of many traditional features of higher education—direct contact with faculty and peers, socialization, networking activities, athletics—and it would not be surprising if these values become available through other means and venues.

It would be absurd to expect universities to wholly abandon their physical plants as they develop Internet-based learning. However, the economics of the model offer a highly attractive for-profit alternative to not-for-profit institutions. The economics may also attract leading faculty, who could find it worthwhile to convert their classrooms for hundreds into electronic classrooms potentially for millions, while being compensated at Michael Jordan salary levels.

We believe that MetaMarkets can and will make a vast contribution to higher education—and that the process will unfold in a way that reasonably resembles the description we have offered. While the process will involve radical change, its purpose is traditional: to increase the overall value of the human capital and intellectual capital in the world. It cannot be denied that, once this trend is under way in earnest, its impact on higher education will be transformational:

- The tenure system is likely to erode: Disintermediation would put students in contact with the best content, developed by outstanding faculty members for electronic classrooms with tens of thousands if not millions of students. The economic foundations of academic careers would change dramatically.

- Many (perhaps most) colleges and universities may find that applications drop precipitously, to the point that their institutions are no longer economically viable.

- The development of instructional and scholarly content would shift to a new model.

- Long tradition and a large, attractive physical plant may become handicaps to institutional leaders attempting to make the leap to MetaCapitalism—yet they could also offer huge advantages for periodic faculty/student counseling, research, and testing beyond online capabilities, if the institutions in question were able to move quickly.

- Exclusivity and the elite status of some institutions would decline in value. Open admissions combined with rigorous competency testing would become the rule for nearly all institutions with electronically mediated offerings.

- There may be a migration of brand value. Brand value would accrue to top "free agent" faculty, the Michael Jordans of the academy. Shareholder value would grow at the intermediary

.com university conferring an accredited degree with courses offered by an all-star, global cast of professors.

All of these trends are under way. Electronic publishing companies are acquiring scholarly journals throughout the world and transforming many of them into online, real-time providers of academic and scientific thinking. Online educational institutions are forming, and large investment funds have been created to develop new models for higher education.

The social and economic results should be truly impressive. Opportunities for higher education will be increasingly available at an attractive price worldwide. When human potential is so widely cultivated, the result should be a dramatic expansion of economic activity on a global basis. Combined with more efficient capital markets, this should have a revolutionary effect on economic value creation and wealth expansion.

The Public Sector

In this discussion we focus on the U.S. public sector only to keep the analysis simpler, but much of the discussion would apply to other governments worldwide. Consuming well over one-third of the nation's gross national product, the U.S. government will be no more sheltered than any other sector from the dynamics of Meta-Capitalism. Disintermediation of the public sector may create large, new privatized segments in the for-profit private sector, organized into service-oriented MetaMarkets.

Whereas e-business is the marketing, buying, and selling of goods and services over the Internet and other electronic media, e-government is the use of electronic information to improve performance, create value, and enable new relationships between governments, businesses, and citizens. E-government builds links between government entities and their customers and suppliers; it connects jurisdictions, customers, units of government, and locations. And in practice, e-government involves taking current government processes and moving them to networks and shared applications.

The federal government has been grappling with e-government for several years—starting with the National Performance Review, which is intended to use e-business to transform the federal procurement process, and continuing with the Access America initiatives (citizen Web access to public services and information). As the public sector has struggled, with varying degrees of success, to apply e-business technologies to its own processes and services, it has sponsored or conducted several pilot exercises with new technologies, including electronic checks, smart cards, and electronic malls. A Presidential memorandum on e-business, dated December 28, 1999, challenged all federal agencies to continue leveraging the Internet to improve customer service and make government processes more efficient and accessible.

State and local governments are moving to the center as they turn their attention to the Internet as a means of improving internal processes, government service, and the flow of information across agencies and jurisdictions. At the conclusion of 1999, more than 50 percent of all states were engaged in e-business initiatives, primarily e-procurement and online tax collection (both targeted at the business community). Many local governments are creating services like ezgov.com, sponsored by Jack Kemp and Mario Cuomo, which brings to the Web basic service providers such as the Motor Vehicle Bureau. The watchword at the local level is to provide citizens "a single window to government" and improved service levels. Figure 5.14 illustrates some recent products.

Governments are taking a modest but effective approach. They are not negotiating large, high-priced contracts to build custom systems from the ground up. Instead, they are deploying small, off-the-shelf solutions to simple, standard problems such as managing the processes required by hunting licenses, property taxes, auto and driver tags, and parking tickets. In classic e-commerce style, these packages are being offered to governments at no cost, in exchange for a piece of the action. For example, if the typical wait-in-line-at-the-DMV process costs the state $7 per transaction and the Inter-

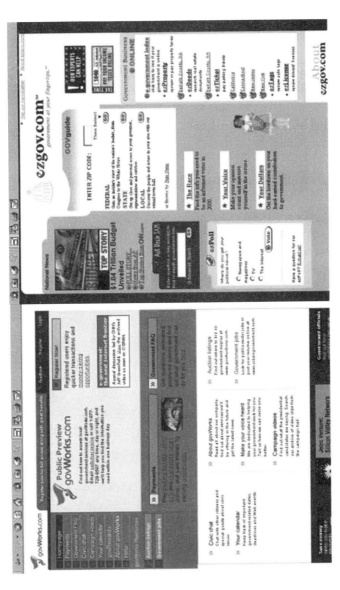

Figure 5.14 Sample government market makers.

net cost is only $3, the company setting up the system charges $1 for each transaction—and everyone comes out ahead.

In addition to providing off-the-shelf solutions to meet a full range of state and local customer interface needs, these e-businesses are operating a variety of government information search engines so that "Netizens" can find their way through what used to be called the maze of bureaucracy. According to Kelly Kimball, chief executive of SDR Technologies, Inc., "The opportunity out there in e-government is so dramatic that even at 200 or 300 percent annual growth, we're falling behind."

The Internet, and its acceptance as a viable business channel, has been the chief driver of accelerated interest in and commitment to e-government among public sector officials over the past six months. Yes, six months—it's new, but it's real and it will be increasingly central to government processes. Key drivers of this transformation include

- Heightened demand for faster, more convenient, more responsive government services from citizens and businesses now accustomed to their expanding online options in the private sector
- A shrinking public sector workforce under continuous pressure to improve, consolidate, or remove paper-driven processes and replace them with electronic processes
- A business community increasingly intolerant of duplicate compliance and reporting requirements and arcane procurement regulations
- Policy makers requiring faster implementation of legislation, who are willing to change law and regulations to enable the broad-based use of electronic technologies

While private sector entities often move to e-business to improve the bottom line, public sector jurisdictions, unconcerned by definition with profit, have their own compelling motivations. Elected and appointed officials wish to build a better public image and achieve superior service. They aspire to increase taxpayer and voter confidence, manage risk and compliance more effectively, and leverage human capital.

Within the next two years, the Internet and other e-technologies will continue to transform government. Some visions of that transformation include a shift in the fundamental role of government agencies from implementer to facilitator. The government's role will be to monitor compliance, as opposed to actively enforcing policy, law, and regulation. Laws will be shaped with real-time public input in light of all relevant historical and statistical data, through the use of online town meetings and e-voting.

As the Internet enables access to timely, consolidated information throughout the ranks of civil servants from top to bottom, government will have an unprecedented view of the performance of service providers and suppliers. Most government processes will become routinized, and the most efficient and effective VAC will provide the service. Government will also serve as a system integrator, MetaMarket creator and manager, bringing together citizens and businesses with the vendors and public employees who serve them. Through an online public service window, citizens will begin to interact directly with end providers such as hospitals, banks, insurance companies, and universities. Requests for service will be electronically routed straight to the provider, without having to move through several layers of government. In response, the service will be provided directly to the requester by the vendor, again bypassing government processes.

Figure 5.15 provides a summary illustration of the transition of government into a MetaMarket construct. The systematic application of the Internet for purchasing and as a service delivery interface creates a MetaMarket in which government services are likely to be increasingly privatized. Many services are overseen by government agencies but not directly delivered by them. (Another possible scenario: The MetaMarket and its VACs might be increasingly overseen by public service market makers in the private sector, i.e., businesses with that mission.) Resulting in part from disintermediation, like other MetaMarkets, the government MetaMarket would offer much more direct interface between citizens seeking government services and private sector service delivery agents.

Over time, those relationships could evolve in interesting ways. For example, parents of children in public schools, home-owners in a neighborhood seeking road maintenance, or citizens seeking municipal fire and police protection might organize to transact directly with private service providers on a performance contract basis. Experiments of this kind in the past have often foundered because of lack of transparency in the delivery system, government disapproval of the quality of services delivered, and the inefficiency of public auctions for the services. Today, the wide acceptance of Net-based approaches provides a dramatic opportunity to decapitalize government, disintermediate services, and create a much more active MetaMarket for public service delivery. The dynamics of the MetaMarket could dramatically improve the performance of service agents within or entering the market, sim-

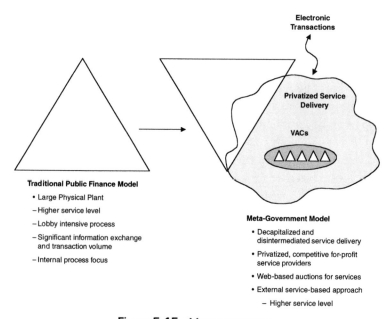

Figure 5.15   Meta-government.

plify the public bidding process, and simplify performance review through rapid consumer feedback. The MetaMarket would also make it much easier to launch new services quickly. It would allow government agencies to focus more attention on citizens and other constituents to assure that service delivery truly meets the needs of recipients.

From an efficiency point of view, such a transformation should dramatically drive down the net cost and growth of public services. By privatizing the delivery mechanism, it dramatically changes the political equation for public services and much of the engine that has driven up the cost of government over the past six decades. It also expands the market-based dimension of public services; heightened competition under MetaMarket conditions will create better service delivery at more attractive prices. Finally, it should disintermediate much of the information and brokerage function of government agencies and dramatically reduce government's need for a large base of physical and human capital.

From a public finance perspective, the economics of private sector Net-based MetaMarkets will hold true: Net-based solutions will create more cost efficiency across the full range of public programs. Privatization and MetaMarket competition in most large programs, including the largest entitlement programs, will look attractive to public finance authorities. Budget reductions on the scale of 20 to 30 percent and increasingly competitive private sector efficiency in delivering public services would mirror the gains offered by MetaMarkets.

The economics will be persuasive on their own, but the political dimension will count. Citizens should demand that public officials

- Aggressively apply MetaCapitalist principles to government
- Reduce public spending by 20 to 30 percent
- Develop public policy frameworks that can respond to an explosive period of economic growth, in which U.S. capital markets valuations may reach $80 trillion in the next 8 to 10 years

Conclusion

There are so many other possible—and, intriguing—ways to illustrate the application of MetaCapitalism. We could describe the disintermediation of health care financing and delivery and the expected portability of health care plans, sold directly to individuals (rather than as a package to corporations) and following individuals from job to job. In other health care sectors, MetaMarkets are forming around the key elements of health care delivery, including medical products supply, imaging and diagnosis, health care financing, and physician management. We could explore new MetaMarkets forming rapidly in the materials and process manufacturing areas. We could look at the major securities exchanges, now attempting to use their information databases to create MetaMarkets across a number of sectors. We could explore the MetaMarkets occurring in pharmaceuticals, utilities, hospitality, and high tech. But the purpose of this book is not exhaustive review. We aspire only to offer a set of strategic principles and insights, supported by conceptual frameworks that should prove useful to managers as they begin to apply the principles.

A dramatic and transformational revolution is under way that reaches across all of our industries, and past them to government. This moment is not unlike the Industrial Revolution. But there is a difference: The Industrial Revolution moved slowly, while this revolution will—in many if not all respects—take place over the next two years, bringing with it gigantic disruptions, opportunities, and the accompanying creation of vast amounts of new economic value and wealth.

While corporate and institutional managers need not understand all of the technical detail or master every aspect of this new revolution, they *will* need to accept massive change rather than ignore it or postpone addressing it. And they will need courage to take part in the revolution and successfully lead their institutions through it.

6

The New Economics of MetaCapitalism and Performance Measurement

Companies participating in the B2C e-business transformation have commanded enormous multiples in the marketplace. Very few of these companies have grown faster than the overall indices, the net profits of many have failed thus far to exceed the companies' cost of capital, and many of the new .com companies, despite their enormously high multiples, have yet to generate a profit. Yet the market continues to reward them.

The markets are not wrong. Real economic value and wealth are being created. An "Internet bubble economy" is not being inflated to the bursting point. And businesses are not simply cannibalizing their own markets or attacking one another's markets within a zero-sum game. At the same time, the basic principles of business still hold. Companies do need to create a sustained flow of profits to be valuable, and year-over-year growth and profitability remain reliable tests of whether or not companies are developing true economic value and creating sustainable wealth. What, then, is the best way to understand the metrics of the New Economy? How best to apply whatever metrics seem credible in order to appraise opportunities and focus investments in areas that will develop value and wealth?

Figure 6.1 asks the key strategic question that should, in our view, be the focus of MetaCapitalist strategies. If the B2C revolution in recent years has generated tremendous value within a very thin slice of the overall economy, how much value will be generated as major icon industrial enterprises transform themselves into MetaCapitalist B2B companies? Perhaps we should keep in mind, as well, the expansion of worldwide capital markets in the past 20 years. This is charted in Figure 6.2.

As Figure 6.2 indicates, global capital market value has increased tenfold over the 20-year period, yielding an annual growth rate of between 13 and 14 percent. On the other hand, the distribution of that market value and wealth has shifted dramatically in the same

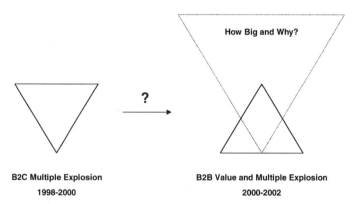

Figure 6.1 The B2B value promise.

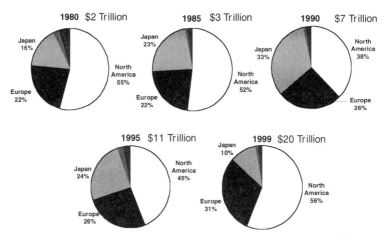

Figure 6.2 The changes in global market capitalization during the 1980s and 1990s.

period. During the 1980s, Japan and other fast-growth Asian countries, as well as West Germany, were able to take advantage of growing global consumer and industrial markets through aggressive export strategies that captured ever increasing market share. The major players from these regions went on to make global capital investments that localized manufacturing overseas and helped to overcome local protectionist sentiment.

Matters were different in the 1990s. As global capital markets were liberalized and integrated, and as network technology began to have a major impact on business performance, the rigidities in Asian economic models and certain European models created a reversal of fortune. This was especially evident in Japan. While Europe's share of overall capital market value expanded, owing to the growing integration of European markets, some European countries—notably the newly unified Germany—went into recession during this period.

Despite regional difficulties, the world as a whole experienced a dramatically consistent and sustained period of growth and expansion, with generally positive social and economic consequences. This predominantly fruitful period may prove to be only a prologue to the potential economic and wealth expansion brought about by the B2B e-business revolution. Throughout this book we have made the point that B2B can accelerate economic growth and value creation from a number of perspectives:

- Expansion of market access
- Better leverage of financial capital
- Significant improvement in operating efficiency
- Dramatic improvement in the efficiency of capital markets
- Mobilization and unleashing of human capital on an unprecedented scale

Assume that the markets are correct and that the capital market response to the B2C Internet revolution is only the beginning of a long-term trend. If this is so, we estimate that the compounded annual capital market growth caused by the new value drivers of MetaCapitalism could accelerate from 13 to 23 percent over the next 8 to 10 years. The graph of this rate of growth, in Figure 6.3, is impressive.

These spectacular results are further illustrated in Figure 6.4, which captures the enormous shifts in world economic conditions that could follow, in our view, from the full unleashing of MetaCapitalism. Economic value creation and wealth creation could increase tenfold over a period of 8 to 10 years, from $20 trillion to $200 trillion. This would naturally generate a multiplier effect: Benefiting from the expansion of consumer and industrial markets, public institutions would have the opportunity to address major global, economic, and societal issues that have resisted solution in the past.

But is this a realistic model of the future? How to understand it from a financial point of view? Analyses that we find convincing suggest that it is actually a conservative model—although the forecasts on which we base our model are already significantly more optimistic than most other published assessments of the impact of the B2B revolution. In general, while some analysts are beginning to point out the potential for greater growth, most do not fully allow for the tremendous multiplier effect created by MetaCapitalism.

Figure 6.3 Growth of global market capitalization 1980–2009.

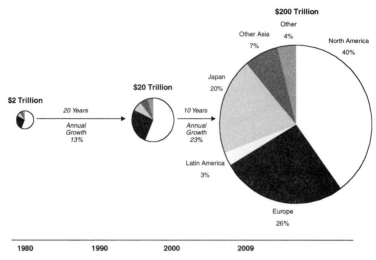

Figure 6.4 Unleashing global value through MetaCapitalism.

Our estimates of worldwide capital market growth will seem reasonable to a few—but to many they will seem unreasonably high. In recognition of the sacred right to doubt, we want to provide some analytic perspective on these growth rates. To give the analysis practical boundaries, we have applied it to only one capital market, the United States. If global capital market value is to accelerate at the rate suggested and reach a valuation of $200 trillion by the year 2009, the U.S. market would need a valuation of at least $80 trillion in market capital by that time. Figure 6.5 suggests the ramp-up to achieve that level of market cap in the United States. The key questions concern the underlying assumptions that would generate that level of market capitalization and the reasonableness of those assumptions.

The analysis begins with a rough estimate of corporate profit growth over this period. Figure 6.6 provides assumptions for underlying nominal gross domestic product (GDP) growth over the period from 2000 to 2009 and projects a possible growth rate of around 6.2 percent. This growth rate is approximately 10 percent faster than in the period from 1986 to 1997—a reasonable assumption in light of the market efficiencies and potential for market

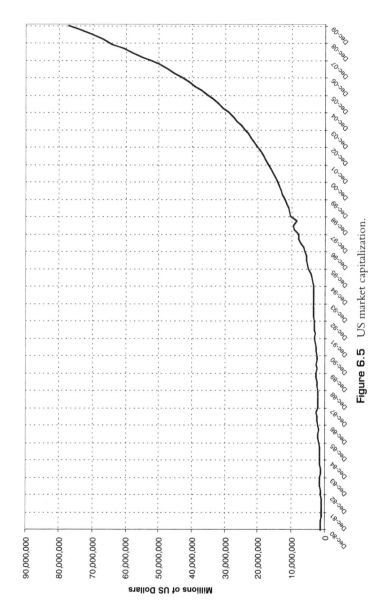

Figure 6.5 US market capitalization.

growth through MetaCapitalism. Some observers go further: They argue that the capacity of MetaCapitalism to respond rapidly to changing market conditions will dampen economic fluctuations, throw off a tremendous amount of cash to support investment and growth, and lead to sustained nominal growth rates well in excess of 6.2 percent. Figure 6.6 charts what such growth would look like.

Figure 6.7 charts the growth rate of corporate profits as a percentage of a GDP growth rate of 6.7 percent over the next nine years. We adjust this growth rate to a level slightly below overall GDP growth, on the premise that the transformations required of companies during this period will be even more dramatic than the process reengineering and globalization initiatives of earlier decades. As a result, growth in corporate profit as a proportion of GDP growth may be somewhat slowed.

Figure 6.8 brings these analyses together to provide overall estimates of corporate profits by 2009. As the figure suggests, corporate profits grow at about 13.1 percent year over year—about the same rate of growth as in the period from 1986 to 1997.

Based on traditional financial analysis as well as the free cash flow models discussed later in this chapter, these numbers are likely to be conservative. Whether fully accurate or conservative, they can now be used to drive the estimate of P/E growth rates charted in Figure 6.9.

The analysis leads to an average P/E ratio of 34 in the year 2009. By comparison, the P/E ratio for the S&P 500 doubled over the last 10 years from 14 to 27. If the P/E ratio were to double over the next 10 years as it did in the last 10 years, it would reach 54 to 56 by the year 2009. If MetaCapitalism truly accelerates value creation, one might expect the P/E ratio to be even greater than 56. However, our analysis generates a P/E ratio of 34, suggesting growth in the P/E ratio at a rate some 60 percent *slower* than in the past 8 to 10 years. Based on this analysis, and in view of analyses offered by other students of the New Economy, we have become increasingly comfortable with a projected P/E ratio of around 34. This, in turn, supports our anticipation of a worldwide capital market expansion to $200 trillion over the next 10 years.

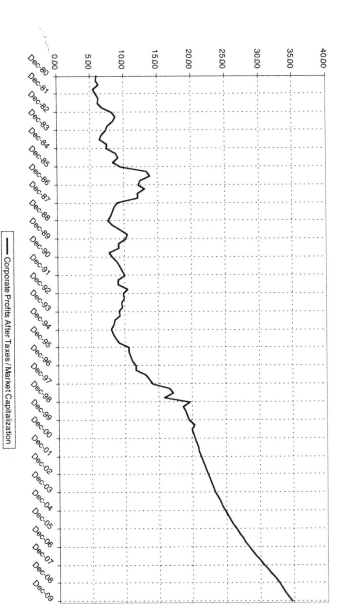

Figure 6.9 US price/earnings ratio.

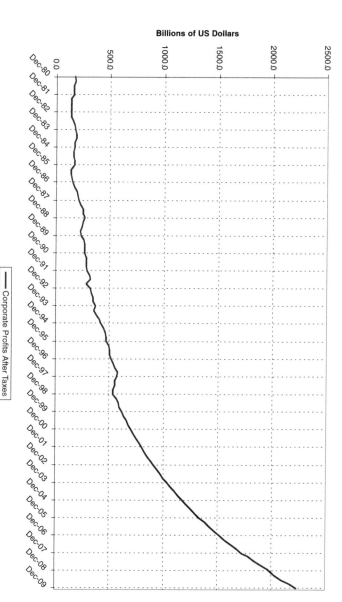

Figure 6.8 US corporate profits.

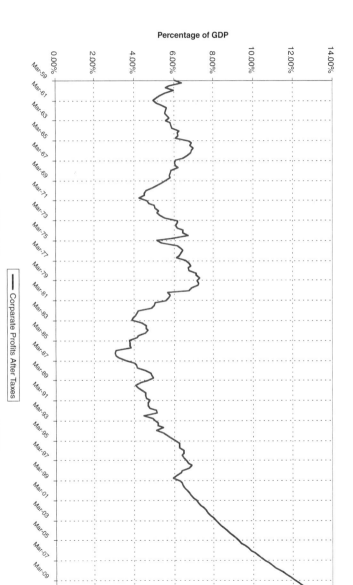

Figure 6.7 US corporate profits as a percentage of GDP.

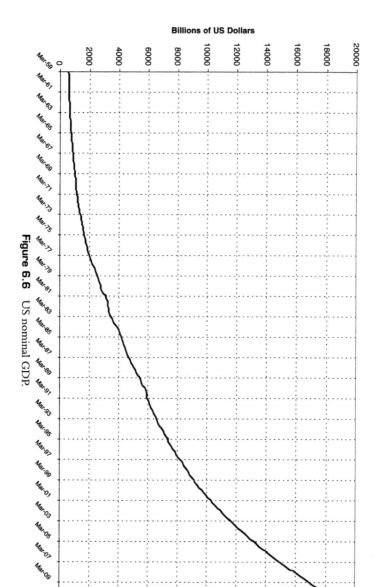

Figure 6.6 US nominal GDP.

Growth acceleration at this rate would dramatically change the most basic assumptions about public finance and the economic well-being of societies worldwide (especially if governments adopt MetaCapitalist models and lower the rate of public spending). If our analysis turns out to be on the mark, entirely new thinking about economic growth, public and private investments, and wealth distribution would be needed.

Some equations explaining the New Economy, created by the Milken Institute, suggest a higher value accelerator due to greater leverage of financial and human capital. Other recent books (e.g., James Glassman, *Dow 36,000,* Times Books, 1999) have suggested that the market did not respond quickly enough to corporate structural and operational changes in the 1980s and 1990s, resulting in an undervalued equity premium. These forecasts project a Dow of 30,000 or 100,000. MetaCapitalism may accelerate these forecasts or even surpass them. There is an enormous leadership challenge just ahead. But meeting the challenge may yield unprecedented results.

Figure 6.10 summarizes selected value drivers of MetaCapitalism. The concepts packed into this figure are worth laying out in sequence:

- Brand-owning companies utilizing electronic channels to customers have the ability to access customers and consumers more rapidly on a worldwide basis.
- The flexibility of electronic channels, plus the decapitalized nature of the brand-owning companies and the dynamics of MetaMarkets, allow brand-owning companies to expand relationships with their customers through rapid introduction of new products and services and greater customer intimacy. These gains, in turn, allow the company to understand customer requirements and needs more quickly, and respond still more satisfactorily in the next cycle.
- The disintermediation of non-value-added processes reduces overall costs and also allows a closer interface between the customer and the supply chain, thus driving additional revenue.

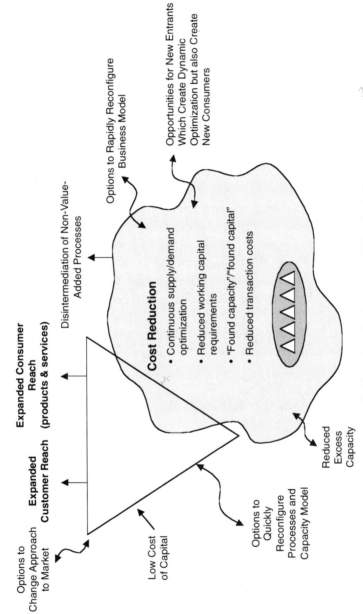

Figure 6.10 Selected value drivers of MetaCapitalism.

- The decapitalized nature of the brand-owning company allows it to shift direction quickly, not only into new markets but also into new sectors. It creates entirely new options for the company in the marketplace.
- The MetaMarket discipline requires continuous financial analysis and reporting. Comparable efficiencies across most basic processes reduce the cost of capital for the principal participants in MetaMarkets.
- Costs are reduced throughout a MetaMarket due to:
  —Continuous supply and demand chain optimization.
  —Reduced working capital requirements.
  —Found capacity and found capital: greater working capital efficiency in MetaMarkets and continuous supply chain optimization allows MetaMarket companies to reconfigure capacity quickly and achieve higher levels of capacity utilization, thus reducing the need for additional capital investment.
  —High-speed communications.
- The dynamic nature of a MetaMarket creates options for the leading players to rapidly reconfigure their business models as market conditions change.
- The free-agent dynamics of a MetaMarket—trading in and trading out players to increase efficiency—drives optimization. It also creates a wider range of new consumers (the employees of successful free agents) who benefit from successful new entrants into MetaMarkets.

The preceding discussion, not intended to be exhaustive, highlights again the range of value opportunities created by MetaMarkets.

As noted earlier, there is a market accelerator in B2B. The growth potential and value of the network is tied to the number of players. MetaMarkets allow enormous numbers of players to enter and leave *easily.* Therefore the value potential of MetaCapitalism is tied to n^2, where n is the number of players in the network, and is accordingly very large for most markets. (By contrast, n is only a few players in a traditional corporate model.) The point behind Metcalf's law is that a network of one fax machine is valueless, while a network of many fax machines creates a huge multiple of value.

From a conventional analytic perspective, MetaMarkets drive opportunities for significant increases in free cash flow and overall operating performance. Thus, you would expect MetaMarket participants to generate higher multiples in the marketplace. In addition, as already noted, their intensive use of electronic channels and their tendency toward continuous optimization allow them to reconfigure quickly to address new market opportunities, all the while improving operating performance. These options need to be factored into the valuation of MetaMarket participants, and they create a needed perspective because static forecasts and pro forma analyses of business performance, absent such resources, will lose their predictive power as MetaCapitalism advances.

Sound strategic planning and financial analysis need both perspectives, the old and the new. They need to understand the impacts of MetaCapitalism from a conventional valuation perspective. They must also address the dynamism of MetaMarkets, their ability to change strategies and operating structures quickly—often in a matter of weeks or months—and thereby generate new value very rapidly. The remainder of this chapter tries to strike a balance between conventional valuation of MetaMarkets and what we take to be the most effective new method: the options-based approach.

The New Economy from a Traditional Perspective

While various theories now compete to explain the superior market rewards for e-businesses, many have at their heart an explicit or implicit assumption that somehow the rules of valuation are moot. In our view the real, profound, and demonstrable business impact of new operating models has not been fully understood. Because the rules of engagement are indeed transforming, familiar free cash flow models have been abandoned—prematurely, we think. Keep them, but complement them with techniques that model and capture the dynamism of MetaMarkets.

What has not yet been well assessed is the effect on B2Cs and B2Bs of established drivers of shareholder value. The main drivers can be conceived as follows:

- Strategies of aggressive decapitalization facilitate higher levels of free cash flow.
- Web-enabled B2B business processes and communities create higher margin potential than traditional business models.
- At marginal economic performance levels, even small incremental improvements in cash operating margins generate a major impact on valuations.

To clarify these observations, consider the comparative assumptions about business models in Figure 6.11. And let's test these hypotheses through the generic example in Figure 6.12. OLDCo is the bricks-and-mortar version of an equivalent e-business-enabled NEWCo. Begin by building a simple, 15-year, free cash flow valuation model for both OLDCo and NEWCo. Our base case assumption is

Free Cash Flow Component	OLD ECONOMY Performance	NEW ECONOMY Performance	NEW ECONOMY Performance Relative to OLD
Operating Cash Flow (EBITDA Margin less Cash Taxes)	Traditional cash margin performance (Avg=2-5% revenue)	Enhanced margin performance due to lower per-unit operating costs	↑ Higher Net Operating Cash Flow
Net Investment in Working Capital	Traditional investment requirements (Avg=1-10% of incremental revenue)	Reduced investment requirements due to faster order-to-cash cycle	↓ Lower Net Investment in Working Capital (possible source of funds)
Net Investment in Fixed Capital	Traditional investment requirements (Avg=1-5% of revenue)	Reduced investment requirements due to single, global e-commerce infrastructure versus physical assets	↓ Lower Up-Front, Capital Investment and Ongoing Maintenance Requirements

Figure 6.11   Business models compared.

Key Value Driver	OLDCo Performance (Yrs 6-10)	NEWCo Performance (Yrs 6-10)	Change Relative to OLDCo Performance	
Revenue Growth Rate	75% - 12% (Avg=38%)	80% - 17% (Avg=43%)	+ 5%	⬆
Cash Operating Margin	5%	7%	+ 2%	⬆
Net Investment in Working Capital	4% - 2% (Avg=3%)	2% - 0% (Avg=1%)	- 2%	⬇
Investment in Fixed Capital	5% - 3% (Avg=4%)	3% - 1% (Avg=2%)	- 2%	⬇
Total Free Cash Flow	($73MM)	$777MM	$850MM	⬆

Figure 6.12   Case study assumptions.

that $200 million in up-front seed capital is committed to each company, and each has identical market prospects and expected cash flows. Each is also presumed to experience rapid growth over its initial business development cycle (years 1 to 5), after which revenue growth fades to recurring growth rates by years 10 to 15.

To estimate the potential market valuation of these firms, we use a traditional discounted free cash flow approach to derive the warranted value of the firms' business plans. The resulting values are a market proxy for the shareholder or equity value of the firms. It can also be argued that this market proxy might be an estimated post-IPO valuation for the firms. For more financially minded readers, we use a no-growth perpetuity assumption to estimate the value of free cash flows occurring beyond year 15 (this is one of the more conservative approaches to estimating residual value).

To assess the value differential between the OLDCo and NEWCo operating model performance, we also flex the NEWCo value driver assumptions based on earlier hypotheses regarding Old Economy versus New Economy performance. As the "Value Staircase" in Figure 6.13 shows, the valuation impacts of even a modest change in performance are quite dramatic.

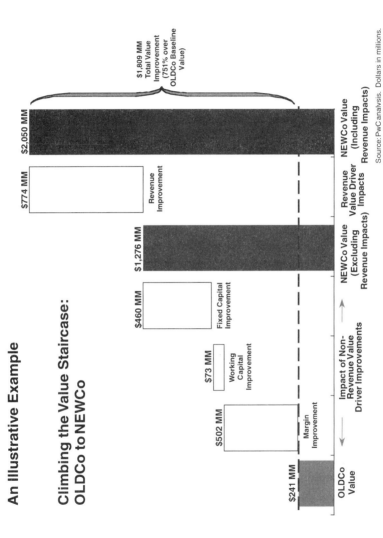

An Illustrative Example

Climbing the Value Staircase: OLDCo to NEWCo

$241 MM — OLDCo Value

$502 MM — Margin Improvement

$73 MM — Working Capital Improvement

$460 MM — Fixed Capital Improvement

$1,276 MM — NEWCo Value (Excluding Revenue Impacts)

$774 MM — Revenue Improvement

$2,050 MM — NEWCo Value (Including Revenue Impacts)

$1,809 MM Total Value Improvement (751% over OLDCo Baseline Value)

Impact of Non-Revenue Value Driver Improvements

Revenue Value Driver Impacts

Figure 6.13 Climbing the Value Staircase: OLDCo to NEWCo.

Source: PwCanalysis. Dollars in millions.

Figure 6.14 applies the analysis to a group of actual NEWCos and OLDCos, and shows how the market actually values them. We selected some of the more preeminent companies from the B2B marketplace as a basis for comparison to Old Economy companies that play in similar marketplaces. Comparing the value/total capital ratios of each of these peer groups, we found that the market is presently providing a valuation premium 5 to 10 times greater to NEWCos than to traditional brick-and-mortar firms. (Remarkably, this result straddles the 8.5 valuation premium in our OLDCo/NEWCo analysis.) For companies with more operating history (five years or more), the valuation premiums fall to the lower end of this range. B2B companies with operating histories of two years or less tend to receive higher valuation premiums, perhaps resulting from the market's euphoria and appetite for the initial share offerings of these firms.

Our conclusion is that the market valuation premiums given to B2B companies are well within the range of what can be expected, given the potential superiority of the B2B business operating model and resultant cash flow value per dollar of capital invested.

Another body of evidence that supports market valuation premiums for B2B companies is recent cash flow trends among the B2C firms. Figure 6.15 shows quarterly cash flow trends for a peer group of New Economy firms, compared to their Old Economy equivalents. The data represent net investment in working and fixed capital per dollar of sales for each of the peer groups. For example, in first quarter 1997, New Economy firms invested $.35 for each dollar of sales reported for the quarter. Old Economy firms had a negative investment (i.e., source of funds) of approximately $.03, because the incremental cost of serving the last customer approaches zero. Scalability brings infinite capacity, reflected in the ratio of cost of assets to next dollar of sales.

As Figure 6.15 suggests, New Economy firms are showing a clear downward trend in the amount of capital required to support higher and higher sales volumes. In this particular data set (which includes Dell, Amazon, Barnesandnoble.com, and Yahoo!), the revenue growth rate over the eight quarters observed was 24 percent

B2B Peer Group Analysis

Sample Companies (25 in Total)	Data Totals	Current Market Cap.	Book Value of Equity	Book Value of Debt	Value/Total Capital Ratio
Ariba, Healtheon, i2 Tech, Sterling Commerce, Commerce One, CISCO, OpenMrkt, VerticalNet, RoweCom, Exodus, DoubleClick, PCOrder, WW Grainger, Chemdex	All Companies (25 Firms)	$788.8	$27.0	$2.1	26.8 to 1
	2 Yrs History or Less (12 Firms)	$67.2	$1.1	$0.1	55.6 to 1
	5 Yrs History or More (8 Firms)	$681.8	$25.6	$1.1	25.5 to 1

Old Economy Peer Group Analysis

Sample Companies (17 in Total)	Data Totals	Current Market Cap.	Book Value of Equity	Book Value of Debt	Value/Total Capital Ratio
Enron, Cabletron Systems, Shared Medical Systems, RR Donnelley, Automated Data Processing, SBC Communications, Sungard Data	All Companies (17 Firms)	$840.1	$99.7	$78.4	4.7 to 1
	5 Yrs History or More (17 Firms)				

On a relative basis, B2B companies can drive higher value-to-capital multiples than comparable bricks-and-mortar firms by more than fivefold.

Figure 6.14 Peer groups compared.

Note: US Dollars in billions, except Value/Total Capital ratios. Market information as of Jan. 26, 2000.

Source: StockSheet.com and PwC analysis.

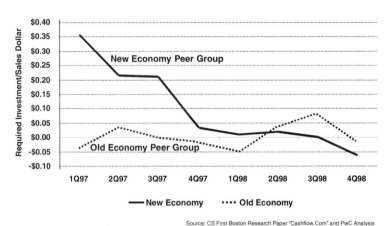

Source: CS First Boston Research Paper "Cashflow.Com" and PwC Analysis

Figure 6.15 The comparison, continued.

quarter-to-quarter, versus 2 percent for the Old Economy peer group. Despite the more than tenfold increase in growth, New Economy firms show increasing capital efficiency. In fact, the most recent quarters show that new capital investment is negative—in effect, a net cash generator for these firms. Old Economy firms, however, show a more stable capital spending cycle without a clear directional trend.

While this data set is limited and trends need to prove themselves over longer periods of time, there is at least a directional indicator that the New Economy business model has superior cash flow generation capabilities.

Real Options in MetaMarkets

To fully understand the value of New Economy companies, free cash flow and related traditional (and still correct) approaches need to be complemented with modeling techniques that capture the financial, human, and brand capital leverage of MetaCapitalism. Real options analysis provides such a framework to assess the value created by the enormous agility, speed, and optimization unleashed in MetaMarkets.

In the Old Economy, a firm was typically valuable because of current cash flow generated from investment capital in a stable business environment. In the New Economy, a firm is valuable not for the stable returns it provides today but because it serves as a platform for generating returns by exploiting a dynamic and unpredictable future. This future is exploited through investments endowed with flexibility or optionality. In the New Economy, future options rather than assets in place or short-term earnings may represent a substantial proportion of a firm's value (see Figure 6.16).

In making investment decisions, CEOs and other executives must realize that management's primary responsibility is still to choose investments that create maximum value for shareholders. That an initiative is based on e-business does not guarantee success. If management's investments can be conservatively defined as attractive options on an uncertain future, then their value is not immediately obvious. Firms are increasingly making high-risk, high-return investments with a limited idea of what the future holds. As a result, the approach to identifying, valuing, and managing investments must change in order to succeed in the New Econ-

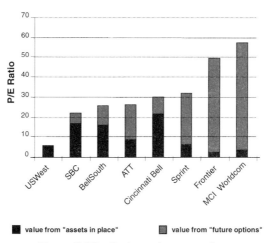

Figure 6.16   Options value comparison.

omy. The new approach must be focused on the future and based on fundamental customer values in addition to rapidly changing market conditions. It must be built on possibilities rather than supposed certainties. In other words, investment options thinking must be incorporated into the new approach.

Given the dynamic nature of the New Economy, the following are some questions that the new approach needs to answer about value creation in the e-business environment:

- What fundamentally do customers value?
- Which e-business initiatives best provide the potential for addressing these fundamental values in the full range of probable futures?
- How can limited resources be allocated to develop an e-business portfolio that maximizes return on shareholder value?
- How should a portfolio of e-business initiatives be monitored and managed over time?

A standard application of the discounted cash flow (DCF) valuation approach answers these questions only approximately. By boiling down all future possibilities to a single scenario and calculating the value of an investment by predicting its payouts, DCF does not adapt optimally to an environment working at e-speed, where an Old Economy month now equals an Internet year. Business leaders need a tool that permits midstream correction—not just once but at many points between the traditional annual episodes of ritualistic strategy and budget formulation.

As typically applied, the DCF approach steers firms away from investments in volatile environments. Higher volatility means higher discount rates and lower net present values (NPVs). Because many of the most promising investment targets today are unable to guarantee definite earnings in the near future, they are often discarded by managers and executives due to their high risk. The DCF model may often lead managers to undervalue the unimaginable and understate the possible value of industries with high uncertainty, such as the Internet. In addition, under the DCF model managers often face obstacles to making NPV-neutral or NPV-negative investments, although such investments are often prerequisite for enhanced research and development. Such investments do not explicitly maximize profits, but by emphasizing past and present earnings, managers who rely on DCF may actually not be maximizing return on shareholder value. In many technology-driven firms, the shortcomings of DCF are commonly known. For example, an executive in a major telecom firm once told us "off-line," "If I believed DCF results, I'd never invest in anything in this business." Of course, his firm does invest—and has a high market valuation as a result of these investments.

Real options theory has emerged as the approach to use in conjunction with DCF in the evolution of valuation techniques. It is becoming a technique of choice in the New Economy. Under this approach, financial options theory and other techniques such as decision theory are combined to help managers understand when a specific nonfinancial value will add positive economic value. Financial options provide a fitting metaphor for this process: Just as financial options have different prices depending on market conditions (e.g., volatility) and terms (e.g., strike price, time to expiration), there are analogs to these market conditions and terms in real options. For example, the price of the real option is the investment required to create it.

The binomial option-pricing model in Figure 6.17 illustrates how options work on a basic, nonmathematical level. The diagram shows how using an option can mitigate and exploit uncertainty. At node A, the initial investment in the option is made. If the investment is a success, the initial return (node B) would be the total amount of the return minus the option price. If the investment is a failure, the initial loss would only be the option price because the option would not be exercised (i.e., the executive would not proceed to the second stage of the investment). The second stage of the investment would be a reiteration of the first. Even if the investment loses money in

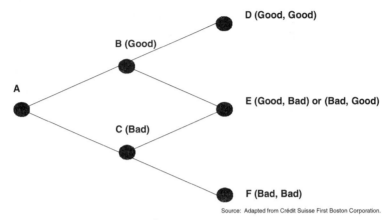

Figure 6.17   Options tree.

both stages, the total loss for the investor is only the sum of the option prices. This allows an investor to absorb more risk while choosing investments with higher potential returns.

In the financial world, options can be priced using very powerful and streamlined tools. The best known tool is the Black-Scholes option pricing model, in which known inputs in financial options have their "real" analogs. For example, in a simple asset acquisition decision, the present value of that asset's free cash flow would be considered the real analog for a financial option of the current value of an underlying stock. Similarly, the expenditure needed to acquire that asset is the "real" equivalent of the strike price of an option in the financial markets. This model also considers the length of time an acquisition decision can be deferred, the time value of money, and the riskiness of the asset's cash flow.

While real options theory allows managers more leeway in choosing their projects, it does not ignore the traditional determinants of value. In many ways, the real world can be more complicated and subtle than the financial world. For this reason, the analytics behind real options theory can become quite complex. Powerful tools and processes are being developed to address these more complex cases.

Despite its largely academic origins, real options theory can be applied in practice to almost any business situation in today's economy. Martha Amram and Nalin Kulatilaka, in a recent article in *Harvard Business Review* ("Disciplined Decisions: Aligning Strategy with the Financial Markets," 1/1/99), note that there are seven common types of real options: timing options, growth options, staging options, exit options, flexibility options, operating options, and learning options. Let's briefly apply this thinking.

A hypothetical example of a timing option would be the decision of Amazon.com about whether to build a book depository in China. Launching the expansion would require a big up-front investment, and it is uncertain whether there is enough demand for Amazon services in the recovering East Asian economy. Amazon has the option of delaying the investment until it conducts further due diligence in the region. To weigh the price of the option is to determine whether the risk avoided by waiting to invest has a greater value than the sales/shipping costs that might be forfeited by postponing construction.

An example of an exit option would be a pharmaceuticals company beginning an effort to commercialize an FDA-approved drug. It has an option to abandon the project if demand doesn't materialize or the liability appears too large.

A direct effect of the growing acceptance of real options theory is a change in investment behavior. By increasing the value of options, real options theory encourages firms to explore different paths in order to accumulate options. Partnerships, alliances, and acquisitions are all different ways to enter a market. Managers become more willing to make major commitments to Internet-enabled businesses because the risk of *not* adapting to the e-business environment is greater than the financial risk of doing so. Further, predictability in an investment is no longer necessarily desired. Because high-return opportunities today are no longer predictable, it is imperative for executives to explore a range of possibilities. Different options strategies can accommodate different investment risk profiles. With options limiting their losses on unsuccessful investments, firms should and will broaden their investment portfolios.

Real options theory suggests that firms can no longer be internally focused in the MetaMarket environment. While some elements of the decision to create or manage a VAC or to become a MetaMarket maker may have obvious value-creating aspects, other aspects of this decision may be largely intangible. Such highly significant intangibles may include increased responsiveness and flexibility vis-à-vis changing market conditions, options on capacity for products and services not yet designed, the structuring of electronic channels to customers when product flow and revenue are insufficient to justify the channel cost, or the acquisition of broadband technology—for example, cable networks—at prices far beyond their current capacity to generate profits and revenue. In these situations it is essential to have a dynamic view of the future and to understand how the dynamics of MetaMarkets will create opportunities around these options as they are exercised.

While complex and uncertain, these alternative futures can be identified and modeled to some degree, and values can be assigned to options created to take advantage of them. The array of options implicit in dynamic MetaMarkets creates such a vast array of futures and options that most senior corporate decision makers are facing decisions on the outer edge of the options frontier, with very high risk/reward ratios. Many can control these risks by initially organizing large purchasing consortia and experimenting with Web-based approaches to managing their businesses. But there will come a point for all major firms in the next two to three years when they will be called upon to make very risky strategic choices in order to maintain leadership in the new world of MetaCapitalism. While new analytic and valuation techniques combined with traditional approaches are helpful, there will be no substitute for aggressive corporate leadership and "change × courage."

7

Bubble In, Bubble Out, Transformation: The Organizational and Change Management Challenge

Clayton Christensen, in his book, *The Innovator's Dilemma* (Harvard Business School Press, 1997), makes the compelling argument that businesses faced with disruptive technologies such as the Internet find it very difficult to redesign and rebuild within their traditional frameworks. Good managers, he argues, are likely to follow their customers' needs and invest where their own return on investment is best—and for these reasons often fail to pursue an emerging technology that has the hidden potential to disrupt their business. Because those technologies tend initially to fall short of their customers' expectations, they seem harmless. In time, however, the technologies progress, their potential is realized, and they surpass existing technologies. Companies that invest in them early—usually start-ups pursuing niche markets—develop a significant lead in the technology and eventually displace the incumbent firms.

Companies tend to avoid innovations when those innovations destroy the value of existing technologies. Change is disruptive. Attempts to produce and sell new products, or to adopt new processes, are inherently disruptive; hence, they meet both political and psychological obstacles. People must learn new ways of doing things, and this takes more time and energy than many are ready to invest. In their own view, they are already working hard, and the increased stress of innovation is often discomforting. As well, the adoption of new processes may retire skills that people have spent years acquiring and honing. Competence-destroying innovations are particularly difficult for companies to adopt. Experience and investments lose value; people are suddenly at risk. Those with influence and position may be threatened by loss of prestige as processes change. Newcomers to the organization may have more value than those who have given their professional lives to it. Younger workers, recently trained at school in the new methods and technologies, may be better able to learn the new processes.

Apart from these individual and organizational dislocations, process and technology changes are costly. Much of the technology and machinery owned by an organization may become worthless. Management is loath to recognize these sunk costs and move on. Moreover, adopting new processes is likely to necessitate new operating systems requiring time, ingenuity, and big budgets to design. Sunk costs, new operating systems—all of this creates a heavy burden and threatens to rob established organizations of the competitive advantages by which they once prospered. Ironically, new firms may be in a superior position because they have no legacy systems that must be scrapped, no traditional organization, culture, and work processes that must be set aside. Owing to these factors, an established company with strong brands and enviable customer relationships and channels of distribution may well lose out to a start-up.

Thanks in part to the persuasiveness and clarity of Christensen's book, major companies are aware of this constellation of challenges, and many are seeking their own transformation. In the context of the New Economy and B2B e-business, corporate transformation will be just as difficult as Christensen predicted—for reasons he foresaw, and for further reasons only now apparent as the B2B e-business revolution advances:

- The business processes of decapitalized, Cisco-like companies are entirely different from the processes of traditional enterprises.
- Designing, organizing, and managing a VAC or MetaMarket is enormously complex and difficult.
- Developing a continuous asset transformation engine (CATE) and using it for continuous improvement requires massive process and cultural changes and greater management discipline.
- MetaMarket businesses require management approaches that are highly dynamic and adaptable, much more organic than conventional approaches.
- Developing highly disciplined and efficient support processes, such as continuous financial reporting, is very difficult.
- The company needs to select a transformational road map and make it effective—for example, incubate new businesses in-house or, alternatively, separate them out at a relatively early stage as new entities.
- Many of the large, installed IT processes and other elements of technical and managerial architecture may not be transferable to the new model.
- Management and staff mindsets, and tools such as performance measurement systems, are tied to the traditional model and not easily transportable to the new model.

- Managing the traditional enterprise to generate cash that will drive the financing of the new-style enterprise is a daunting management task. Companies will try.

Yet some models of the transition are already unfolding. Automotive companies are building their Internet purchasing and delivery systems on the backs of their current fulfillment systems, and most of the transactions are conducted in traditional dealerships so that delivery, sales and servicing, and ongoing servicing can be set up appropriately. Similarly, e-retailers are using some of their traditional wholesale and retail distribution backbone to support the new Internet-based sales channel. Companies in all industries are moving to develop market-making businesses—that is, taking their first steps toward MetaMarkets.

These varied efforts to transform companies from traditional companies to MetaCapitalist companies generate a vast array of questions with regard to project management and, more broadly, change management. We chart the basic steps of the transformational process as follows:

1. Determine the right MetaMarket vision for the industry and for the company. It must generate maximum profitability as well as options-related value.
2. Understand how to outsource successfully, control the VAC and MetaMarket network, aggregate customers, sustain stable customer relations and customer access channels, avoid excessive pricing arbitrage, and set up a business plan that will generate superior returns and profit as well as year-over-year growth.
3. Systematically manage the outsourcing and insourcing of a large proportion of physical capital and noncore processes.
4. Create process models and organizational structures to fit the MetaMarket.
5. Develop the technology infrastructure to interface among the brand-owning entities and the VACs.
6. Develop the new management strategies, tactics, and metrics required to create a successful B2B company.

A key question is this last one: How will management organize to drive this transformation? We believe that the process will be much like the Quality initiatives and Six Sigma transformations of recent decades. Management will take a strong leadership role. It will decide to pursue the B2B model and direct the company to that approach rather than wait for endless reviews of all alternatives. Aggressive management teams at General Electric, Ford, Honeywell International, and IBM, among other successful companies, have adopted a vision of the B2B e-business future, and they are driving their companies to get "from here to there" in the least possible time.

As suggested in Figure 7.1, we expect the most successful corporate transformations to occur when the CEO adopts the MetaMarket vision on the right-hand side of the chart and tasks management teams to move the company rapidly toward it. Essentially, the CEO would define the right-hand side as the strategy and task various teams to create projects in areas such as these:

- Internal e-processes: procurement, other supply chain, financial accounting, HR, R&D, engineering, and so on.
- VAC and MetaMarket development: processes, technology, alliances, new internal process models, and overall business model.
- Operations outsourcing, including strategic procurement, manufacturing, and service provision. Each project to be accompanied by cost reduction and performance improvement metrics. If and when successful, these projects will free up additional capital to focus on product development and customer management projects.
- Distribution outsourcing, plus the creation of new processes to manage customer delivery and fulfillment channels from the outsourced network to the consumer.
- New applications of e-R&D and e-product development to bring products to market faster, leverage the company's intellectual capital, and gain rapid access to intellectual content outside the company through the Internet.

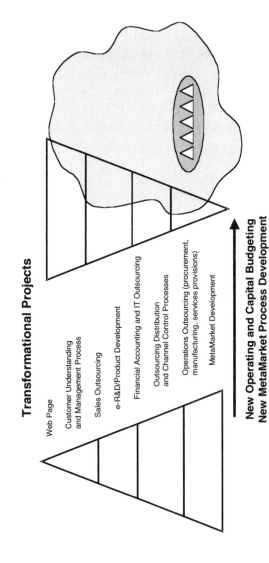

Transformational Projects

Web Page

Customer Understanding
and Management Process

Sales Outsourcing

e-R&D/Product Development

Financial Accounting and IT Outsourcing

Outsourcing Distribution
and Channel Control Processes

Operations Outsourcing (procurement,
manufacturing, services provisions)

MetaMarket Development

**New Operating and Capital Budgeting
New MetaMarket Process Development**

Figure 7.1 Directed change management approach for MetaCapitalism.

- Outsourcing of financial accounting, selected IT systems, and other support functions.
- The creation of external customer interfaces, web pages, and the launching of new customer understanding and management processes; perhaps, as well, the outsourcing of various sales and marketing functions.
- Creation of a CATE to drive change and keep pace with changes occurring in the MetaMarket in terms of product, organization, and process.

The strategic planning process would be tasked with creating projects that move the company to a new business model over a short period of time—no more than 18 months to three years. Metrics would be put in place to measure the short-term effect and success of the projects (for example, cost reduction and more rapid throughput), and new metrics would be developed for the emerging MetaMarket business (see Chapter 3). Throughout the execution of these projects, new business processes would be designed and implemented along the lines suggested by the B2B process model in Figure 3.8.

As teams executed these projects, the enterprise would slowly develop a broad understanding of the new business model and reach consensus as to its strategic attractiveness. New leadership for the B2B model would be identified among the leaders of project teams. This overall approach to change management would successfully apply the core concepts of effective change management—understanding, consensus building, and the development of a clear transformational road map. In our view and experience, it provides part of the solution to the innovator's dilemma.

Bubble In, Bubble Out, and Transformation: Converting to MetaCapitalism

Our research has demonstrated that three distinct approaches can be used to create an e-business. The first we call Bubble In: organizing the e-business effort completely within an existing enterprise. The second is Bubble Out: organizing the effort as a separate entity free from the parent company's cultural and organizational constraints. And the third is Transformation: completely reinventing the existing organization as a Web-based enterprise.

The traditional methodology for designing organizations involves a top-down approach with a well-developed corporate strategy driving the organizational structure. But this time-tested approach may not be fully applicable in the evolving electronic economy. A key aspect of the New Economy is rapid and constant change, requiring organizations to be extremely flexible and responsive. In Microsoft Chairman Bill Gates's oft-quoted words, "If the 1980s were about quality and the 1990s were about reengineering, then the 2000s will be about velocity." Our research shows that some common characteristics are needed for the successful development of an e-business organization in such an environment.

One key condition is an entrepreneurial environment very similar to that of a start-up organization. At the heart of the organization's capabilities should be the ability to improvise where needed, make quick but sound decisions with limited information, support risk taking, and even fail without disastrous consequences. When there is a failure, the organization should be able to learn from its mistakes, quickly adapt, and move on. We are describing a laboratory-like environment that encourages free experimentation with new ideas. Are we, therefore, predicting the demise of corporate strategy? Not at all—but a more flexible approach to organizing and guiding businesses will be necessary in the New Economy. The organization must be free to reinvent itself as multiple strategic opportunities emerge (see the discussion of real options in Chapter 6).

Fluidity, adaptability, innovation, improvisation—how best to create and sustain these traits? Our response to this question reflects the three distinct approaches:

- *Bubble In:* The parent organization creates a laboratory-like environment to incubate e-businesses. In such an environment, the bureaucratic constraints of the parent are kept at bay. The new entity is an autonomous skunk works, operating with senior management's blessing and protection.

- *Bubble Out:* The parent organization creates an environment outside of itself in which the new entity can grow and thrive. When an organization adopts this model, it can choose to create a new entity connected to the existing structure (example: Wells Fargo) or form an entity that is entirely different from the parent organization (example: WingspanBank.com, created by BankOne). We call these two approaches *Extension* and *Segregation,* respectively. In the end, the new unit may consume the traditional business or spin off.

- *Transformation:* The organization reinvents itself by making all customer-facing, internal, back-end, and enterprise processes Web enabled. In the resulting structure, the parent organization is subsumed by the e-organization.

The three models are shown graphically in Figure 7.2.

Companies can move from one model to another or even combine various aspects of the three models. For example, in cases where the parent organization is able to create an internal incubator for nurturing e-business, eventually the initiative will probably become larger and more visible to others in the parent organization. The initiative may then generate resentment and friction over such issues as resource allocation and culture. Once this situation occurs, the parent organization may have to restructure the e-business as an external entity.

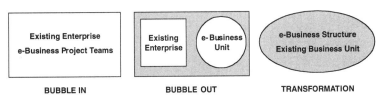

Figure 7.2   MetaCapitalist corporate transformation.

The debate about whether brick-and-mortar businesses will be replaced by Web-only businesses has been more or less settled. Most analysts agree that traditional organizational forms will coexist with virtual ones, if only to provide some degree of "touch and feel" for end users. This is acknowledged even in the retail industry, which has been subject to the severest onslaught in the New Economy. Retailers have discovered that a mixed channel or "click and mortar" strategy is best for them. Hence, transformation in their industry, as in many others, need not mean a complete teardown of the traditional business. Traditional businesses will exist as part of larger, e-enabled structures.

To clarify the concepts of Bubble In, Bubble Out, and Transformation, we summarize their characteristics in Table 7.1.

The best approach for a given company depends on two key measures. The first is the degree to which the organization is already endowed with enablers for e-business. How readily will it adapt to an e-business environment? The second measure is the degree of uncertainty created by the New Economy for that particular company. How great is the risk incurred by the company if it does not adapt to the new environment?

e-Business Enablers

The first measure can be broken down into enabling factors needed for an effective e-organization. An organization can be said to possess a high degree of enabling factors—in other words, adaptability—if it is

- Oriented toward information and knowledge sharing
- Entrepreneurial
- Responsive and agile
- Nonbureaucratic and nonhierarchical
- Creative and original
- Collaborative
- Risk-tolerant, even risk-encouraging
- Decisive, even when lacking information
- Proactive

Table 7.1 Characteristics of Three Organizational Models for e-Business

Characteristic	Bubble In	Bubble Out	Transformation
Location of e-initiative financials • **P&L statements** • **Budgets**	Within an existing unit of the parent company (e.g., IT or finance).	Outside the existing organization, in a newly defined e-entity.	Parent company financial statements and budgeting reflect financial performance (e.g., ROI, margins) associated with leveraging e-commerce.
E-initiative executive reporting structure	Within an existing unit of the parent company (e.g., e-initiative leader reports to someone *outside* senior executive management).	New reporting structure attached to current parent company, e.g., e-initiative leader reports to someone *inside* senior executive management (CEO, COO).	Executives charged with e-initiative responsibilities will have seats on senior executive management committee.
E-initiative staffing roles & responsibilities	Staff have matrix roles, responsibilities, and reporting within current organization *and* new e-initiative.	Staff have new roles, responsibilities, and reporting *only* within new e-initiative.	Organization redesigns roles and responsibilities across value chain to leverage disintermediary effects of e-commerce.
E-initiative degree of autonomy	Strategic decisions depend on overall direction of parent company. The e-initiative competes with other parent-company initiatives for infrastructure and resources.	Strategic decisions are made *only* within e-initiative. Unit is completely autonomous to make infrastructure and resource decisions. Parent company may retain branding control and year-end profit-taking.	E-initiative *is*, increasingly, the company and occupies center in strategic decision making.

Note: Bubble Out can range from an extension of the existing organization to a segregated unit formed through acquisition, spin-off, or other developments.

These characteristics capture the essence of the laboratory-like, entrepreneurial environment that is needed for an e-business to thrive. Taken together, they represent the extent to which the organization is already like a successful e-business in its culture, management practices, and infrastructure. A company strong in all these measures is likely to adapt to changing environments without missing a beat. The further along an organization is, by these measures, the easier it will be to incubate a new entity within itself or even

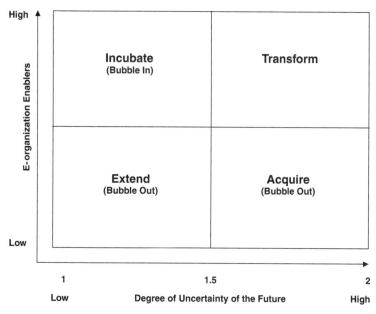

Figure 7.3 Strategy selection: first matrix.

transform itself. However, few if any organizations have evolved at the same pace and to the same extent in all of these respects.

Degree of Uncertainty Created by e-Economy

The second measure for determining the best model is the degree of uncertainty created for the organization by the New Economy (see Figure 7.3). It looks at the options and opportunities of adapting to the new environment. This measure is affected by factors such as these:

- Business model compatibility
- Operational compatibility
- Industry structure
- Clockspeed

In the emerging electronic economy, many traditional, brick-and-mortar business constraints become irrelevant. Hence, the business model should be designed to offer *all* the relevant products in its domain, unconstrained by any barriers whatever. Consider the example offered by Wal-Mart. In its traditional stores, the company's advanced technology infrastructure helps it offer a profit-maximizing mix of products at profit-maximizing prices. However, a key constraint is available shelf space; the Wal-Mart business model of maximizing profits is subject to this physical constraint. On the other hand, shelf space in the virtual world is unlimited. There are no constraints on what consumers are offered and can buy—or at least there need be none. The e-business model can focus on providing ease of search and location, quick fulfillment of customer orders, and complementary or related product presentation and cross-selling. Finally, Wal-Mart has the beginnings of a VAC in its collaboration with Fingerhut and Books-A-Million.

In summary, we won't hesitate to state the obvious: The more compatible the existing business model with the emerging B2B e-business model, the less the organization must change to succeed in the New Economy. Identically, if its operations are compatible with the emerging operational model for e-business—for example, using one intranet or many to bind the company together—only minimal changes will be needed to make a successful transition to e-business.

Clockspeed

The new concept of clockspeed refers to the rate of evolution of different industries. It is gaining importance in the New Economy. There are three dimensions to explore—product clockspeed, organizational clockspeed, and process clockspeed:

- *Product clockspeed* measures the life span of product families. For example, Intel microprocessor product families have a typical market life of two to four years.
- *Organizational clockspeed* measures the turbulence of organizational dynamics. This can be assessed through the intervals

MetaCapitalism

between CEO transitions, organizational restructurings, ownership changes, and the like. For example, organizational boundaries are repeatedly redrawn in the media and entertainment industry, owing to mergers, acquisitions, divestitures, and other forms of organizational change.

■ *Process clockspeed* measures the rate of evolution of new processes. For example, automobile companies expect that a billion-dollar investment in an engine or assembly plant will remain productive for 20 years or more. In the Internet economy, features such as 24 × 7 capabilities and seamless global trading have greatly increased clockspeeds in several industries, thus posing new challenges and uncertainties.

Tools such as scenario analysis facilitate the evaluation of potential uncertainties that the New Economy may impose on an organization. It will come as no surprise that the two measures we have focused on—e-organization enablers and the degree of uncertainty—construct handily into a series of matrices, among them Figure 7.4. This figure condenses a good many factors and possible scenarios into a single pattern, as follows:

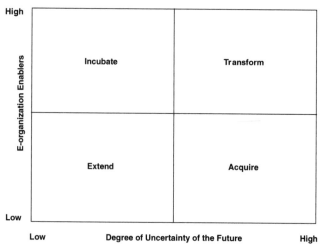

Figure 7.4 Strategy selection: second matrix.

- *Incubation.* When the organization is already endowed with a high level of enablers, and the electronic economy does not pose too many uncertainties, it should proceed into e-business right away by incubating a new unit within the existing framework.
- *Transformation.* When the organization has many enablers and the risk of doing nothing is high, the organization should completely reinvent itself. Doing so should be fairly painless; not doing so is likely to incur a heavy penalty.
- *Acquisition.* If the organization has few enablers and a high degree of uncertainty, it is imperative to change drastically. Doing so internally would involve great organizational upheaval.
- *Extension.* When the degree of uncertainty is low but the organization has few e-commerce enablers, internal organizational barriers are likely to be holding the company back.

How does the matrix address the question of the best model—the model that will best serve a specific company's needs? If it earns a place in the Incubate quadrant, an organization is intrinsically ready to take the plunge into e-business. The environment, however, does not force such an organization to be in any particular hurry. The appropriate approach is Bubble In, whereby the organization uses an internal laboratory to develop e-business capabilities.

In the Transform quadrant, the risk associated with not adapting quickly to the electronic economy is very high. However, the organization is also endowed with a high level of adaptability. Hence the appropriate model is Transformation.

In the lower two quadrants (Extend and Acquire), the organization is unlikely to be able to support either a complete transformation or an internal incubator. For this reason, it must turn to external means of enabling itself for e-business (Bubble Out). If the degree of uncertainty is low, then the new organization can be set up as an extension of the existing organization. On the other hand, if there is substantial risk associated with continuing inside the existing organization, the new entity should be segregated to minimize conflict. We summarize our conclusions in the matrix shown in Figure 7.5.

Organizations may migrate through one or more of these three approaches before settling on what is best for them. Consider Charles Schwab, a major discount broker. In its endeavor to become e-enabled, it started with a Bubble In approach—perhaps on the premise that it had the requisite enablers and the uncertainty posed by the Internet economy was low. However, once the e-business operation grew to about 30 people, and it could no longer be overlooked as a skunk works project, incompatibilities with the existing organization began to appear. It had to be *segregated* and permitted to grow without artificial constraints on its potential. As the now-external Internet unit grew phenomenally, the parent organization completely changed its view of e-business. The Internet unit was then brought back into the parent organization, which rapidly transformed itself into a multichannel provider. At last look, Internet operations were providing well over half the company's trading volume.

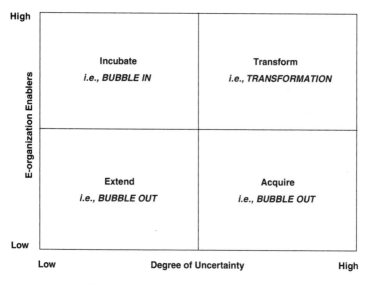

Figure 7.5 Strategy selection: third matrix.

Where to Start?

The first step in developing an e-business initiative is to decide where to focus. In general, the appropriate focus is the entire organization, but in the case of large, multidivisional enterprises, the relevant focus could be just one business or a set of linked businesses. Divisions within the same company may well exhibit different characteristics and hence need to be treated as different units for analysis—for example, the Saturn division of General Motors is likely to be substantially different from other divisions. As a general rule of thumb, parts of an organization that have their own P&L responsibility should be treated as different units. Even when the P&L responsibility is not distinct, if a certain part of an organization is distinct in other respects, such as products, markets, or organizational culture, it should be treated as a separate unit for purposes of analysis.

Once the appropriate unit of analysis is established, it will be possible to define not only those qualities that are likely to enable e-business but also the uncertainties posed by the New Economy for that particular unit. This analysis can be quickly enough completed, with the use of the diagnostic tools we propose in this book. A more detailed analysis, using tools such as scenario analysis, would throw further light on the organization's position in the e-business matrix. Once the organization's position in the matrix is clear, the decision whether to Bubble In, Bubble Out, or try other options is within reach. That decision, in turn, may lead to explorations along the lines proposed in earlier chapters: to found a VAC of e-business partners, to take steps toward the creation of a Meta-Market. Then the twenty-first century has dawned not only on the calendar page, but in the company.

Epilogue

A New World: Closing the Digital Divide

This book has traced dramatic changes that will soon begin in earnest and create a vastly altered business landscape. While we have focused on business economics, this scenario has major implications for the world's political economy—for how people live and the opportunities available to them. Figure E.1, drawn from the valuation analysis in Chapter 6, reflects a possible—and desirable—world of the year 2009, in which enormous wealth and economic value have been created by an essentially New Economy and technology. One of its brightest features is that it offers virtually equal opportunity for participants worldwide. This forecast suggests recovery in Japan, combined with significant growth in other parts of Asia and Latin America. These gains will somewhat reduce the worldwide share of capital market value in Europe and North America. However, with the total economic pie growing by a factor of 10 in the course of the next eight to nine years, there should be more than enough to go around.

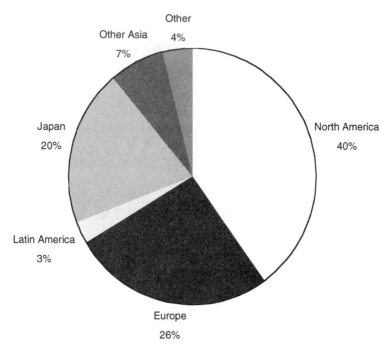

$200 Trillion

Figure E.1   Market capitalization 2009.

On a global basis, the ability of MetaCapitalism to leverage economic and human capital will allow countries in some of the poorer neighborhoods of the world to make gigantic strides. Significant among these should be countries such as Russia and India, with enormous populations of highly educated, technology-minded citizens who are, at best, underemployed in the current worldwide economic system. The principal problem they face is that the financial and physical infrastructures of their countries are inadequate to leverage their skills. Difficulties of various kinds at the level of the nation—political, economic, and financial confusion, restrictive public policy, and other factors—have slowed the development of an effective policy structure and strategy to address their needs.

The New Economy may be what they are waiting for. Over the next few years, MetaMarket frameworks and infrastructures will allow businesses anywhere in the world to bid for opportunities to participate in industry supply chains or to contract for outsourcing many processes such as financial accounting, software maintenance, and human resources transaction management. Because the electronic infrastructure underlying these new relationships will be increasingly integrated worldwide, location becomes irrelevant. Entrepreneurs in Moscow, Calcutta, Warsaw, Taipei, Mexico City, and Buenos Aires can create businesses linked to the worldwide network through any manner of broadband channels and become full participants in dynamic MetaMarkets. Traditional infrastructure constraints—ports, railroads, roads, and even local financial systems and capital markets—will become far less relevant in this New *Meta*-Economy, which will leapfrog many such traditional constraints and in many cases requires only e-infrastructure that is relatively easy and quick to build.

The new world of MetaCapitalism creates a new set of critical success factors for winning and growing:

- Sufficiently strong network infrastructure (relatively easy to obtain but requiring the political will to liberalize policies) and easy network access for the country's businesses and consumers.
- Local capital markets fully integrated into worldwide capital markets, facilitated by easy network access from any point worldwide.
- Relatively low levels of economic nationalism, with minimum restrictions on the inflow and outflow of goods, services, and information.
- Relatively open internal capital markets, allowing investment capital to flow freely to ventures that might provide a high rate of return in an economy organized increasingly around MetaMarkets. If capital flow is restricted due to public policy or informal (cartel-like) corporate alliances and agreements, the dynamic optimization possible through

MetaMarkets will not occur. MetaCapitalism is about business, but it is also and very powerfully about the interface between government and business—and people's lives and welfare are at stake.

Countries that have adapted to the worldwide changes of the 1990s (democratization, privatization, global capital markets, and the lowering of capital, trade, and other barriers) will be the biggest winners in the new MetaCapitalist world. Within those countries, there will be many successful business start-ups. But large, established companies will not be left behind—particularly if they have accepted and implemented the highly significant waves of change that occurred in the past 20 years: process redesign, supply chain synchronization, time-based competition, global strategies supported by global networks, and investments in PC network technology. Countries in which companies have adopted ERP and CRM solutions, with some of the associated standardization of business processes, will also most easily adapt to the technology infrastructure of MetaCapitalism.

Figure E.2 identifies countries that may be quite well prepared for these transitions, and others that may experience sharp increases in growth and major economic opportunities. On the other hand, countries that continue to maintain restrictive economic and policy structures may make the transition difficult, and others face a future that could turn either way—they are poised on the edge with highly uncertain futures. This chart will raise questions; we are well aware that it is subject to debate. In many respects, we hope it is wrong. But from our present perspective, this is what we see.

The countries that can in all fairness be regarded as ready for the New Economy tend to be those that have adopted network technology and achieved widespread technology access. They have gone through the most significant capital market restructurings and liberalizations of the past 10 years. And they demonstrate a high level of new enterprise formation alongside traditional enterprises committed to leadership in the next century.

By contrast, countries that can justly be viewed as facing a dif-

Relatively Prepared	Difficult Transition	Major Opportunities	Uncertain
US	Germany	Russia	Brazil
UK	Japan	India	Mexico
France	China	Eastern Europe	Korea
Italy	Indonesia	Singapore	
Benelux	Malaysia	Taiwan	

Figure E.2 Comparative preparedness for MetaCapitalism.

ficult transition tend to have been slower to liberalize their capital markets. They often maintain formal and informal vertical capital distribution structures (e.g., cartel/*kereitsu*-style), and they practice some degree of economic nationalism in terms of restricting trade flow, capital investment, and corporate restructuring. Some maintain restrictions on enterprise development and expansion.

Countries with significant opportunities may have highly technical but underutilized educated populations. The most entrepreneurial among them could form businesses, create work for many others, and actively compete in MetaMarkets with a minimum of new enterprise investment.

Finally, countries where uncertainty reigns tend to have well-developed business infrastructures, but their overall economies are going through major transitions. They have more than their fair share of risks to confront.

Nonetheless, *all of the countries* should see significant economic expansion and growth during the next nine years; all should benefit tremendously from the promise of MetaCapitalism.

This throws open the remaining question posed by this book. What are the societal and public policy implications of a global economy that has made the transition of the millennium from a focus on *economic necessity* to a new era of *economic surplus?* This is not an easy question. It is certainly an exciting one and brings with it huge opportunity for human progress.

e.nough

Index